Made for Manhood

A Course in Christian Adventure
For Fathers and Sons

TELEO SCOUTS
Completion In Christ

Winters Publishing
P.O. Box 501
Greensburg, IN 47240
812-663-4948
www.winterspublishing.com

TELEO SCOUTS
Completion In Christ

Acknowledgments

Gratitude is expressed toward several key people without whom this publication would not have been possible:

To my wonderful wife, Shireen, who graciously allowed me to interrupt her countless times when I needed editorial audience. Your encouragement and inspiration have been amazing.

To my sons, who have been a constant source of inspiration and joy. I am so proud of each of you!

To the terrific dads who have been part of my own Teleo Scouts chapter. You all impress me beyond description.

Thanks especially to Phil Duran, whose encouragement rekindled an idea in perfect time.

To Jeff Stonerock, who challenged me so many years ago to become complete in Christ, and in doing so showed me how in both word and deed.

To Mike Riness, who taught me how to put my faith into practice for the long haul.

To Jesus Christ, our Salvation and Completer.

Please visit our website for information regarding Teleo Scouts:
www.teleoscouts.com

For information regarding speaking engagements, training, or publicity, please contact Teleo Scouts at (231) 539-7773.

Table of Contents

Introduction

What is Teleo Scouts?

Teleo Scouts was created with both fathers and sons in mind. It is our central conviction that there is no better way for boys to be raised into manhood than through the godly influence of loving and involved fathers.

In Teleo Scouts, like-minded men join with their sons for the purpose of mutual adventure and godly learning. *Made for Manhood* provides an array of lessons which promote character development and an adherence to a Christian worldview. In addition to the lessons, fathers and sons engage in a variety of activities together. The agenda for the activities is set forth by the group according to its own, unique interests.

What does *Teleo* Mean?

Teleo is a Greek word which signifies completion. It is for this reason that the phrase *"Completion in Christ"* is displayed throughout much of Teleo Scouts' printed literature.

The Teleo Scouts' Curriculum

The Teleo Scouts' curriculum is comprised of three

components:

1. *Made for Manhood*—This is the text you are presently holding. It is primarily used as the central part of the Teleo Scouts' curriculum for young men, but it can also be enjoyed as a personal study guide or as a discipleship resource for an older audience.

2. The *Parents' and Leaders' Manual*—This text is a complement for the lessons found in *Made for Manhood*. It contains guidelines and tips for parents and youth leaders on how to present the content and be part of a Teleo Scouts chapter.

3. The *Folio of Merit Awards and Resource Guide (optional)*—This kit provides high quality, reproducible prints of all available Merit Awards, along with their respective criteria for advancement. The resource guide provides appropriate help and advice.

Forming a Teleo Scouts Chapter

A Teleo Scouts representative is available to provide training or to answer any questions related to beginning a chapter. The representative can provide curriculum materials for your group as well. Call 231-539-7773 for any inquiries in this regard.

Once two or more Christian men determine they want to form a Teleo Scouts' group, they simply inform The Teleo Scouts' main office of their intent. Each member will want to review the *Statement of Beliefs* and *Membership Requirements* to ensure that the spirit and integrity of the program is maintained.

The Group Leader

One of the men in the chapter acts as its leader. The leader's primary role is to organize the schedule of the group. The *Parents' and Leaders' Manual* provides guidelines and instruction for carrying out this enjoyable role. The other men, along with the leader, take turns facilitating the events of the schedule.

Group Meetings

A local chapter meets as little or as often as it likes. A recommended starting point is twice a month. After some time, the group may determine that it wants to meet more or less often.

Meetings consist of a lesson from *Made for Manhood* and an activity planned by the men.

Lessons

The lessons are provided in *Made for Manhood*. All group members are encouraged to read and review an assigned lesson before meeting time. During meetings, the lesson is presented and taught by one of the fathers. The other fathers in the group may also offer their wisdom and insight during the lesson as they deem appropriate. This "plurality of leadership" is a powerful and effective way to speak into the lives of the young men.

The lessons will take about a year to cover in their entirety, depending on how often the group meets.

Activities

The group's activities are designed and planned by the various men in the group, each taking turns in a manner that best suits their schedule.

Activities can reflect the diverse backgrounds and talents of the fathers, or they may reflect new interests that the group would like to experience together. Regardless, these activities provide hands-on learning and rich memories that produce well-rounded young men.

An activity may take place before or after a lesson, however it best suits the group. The *Parents' Manual* offers an extensive list of possible activities for consideration.

In Addition….

Teleo Scouts also has an optional Merit Award program available for those interested.

Merit Awards address a wide variety of topics, ranging from physical fitness to various academic pursuits. There are seven phases that a young man may advance through, each one slightly more challenging than the prior.

Details of the Merit Award program are found in the *Folio of Merit Awards and Resource Guide* for those who want to consider this component of the curriculum.

Additional suggestions and guidelines for organizing local chapters are offered in the *Parents' Manual*.

Orientation

You are about to embark on an adventure called Teleo Scouts. It is called "Teleo" because *teleo* is a Greek word which means complete, accomplished, well-rounded, and finished. And it is called "Scouts" because you will be sent forth to discover and accomplish great things.

Teleo and Its Use in the Bible

Jesus used the word *teleo* when He declared, "I have finished (*teleo*) the work which thou hast given me to do" (John 17:4).

The great apostle Paul also used the word *teleo* when he stated, "I have fought the good fight, I have finished (*teleo*) the course, I have kept the faith" (2 Tim. 4:7).

In both of these examples, it is apparent that these great men had already accomplished much of their lives' missions, while you have only recently begun yours. But this doesn't mean that you can't envision your life as one day also being complete. On the contrary, we should all make it our highest aim to finish the course of life as did the great men who have gone on before us!

Teleo and Its Meaning for You Today

So then, you can begin to think of yourself as a scout who

is on his way to becoming complete. To what degree you will become complete is largely up to you, but it is sufficient to say that you will be closer to completion each step of the way than you were before you set forth.

What does it mean to be "complete" and "well-rounded"? For starters it means that you are a Christian, for no man can ever hope to be complete without aligning himself with God's holy Son. For this reason you will see the phrase *Completion in Christ* in much of the printed literature associated with Teleo Scouts.

Aligning yourself with Jesus Christ is vital to being a real man, and so it bears repeating: No man can be complete without Christ. Many men have tried to be real men without Christ, and each has failed in his folly.

Jesus said a man without Him is like a branch without a vine. A man without Christ might also be likened to a ship without a sail, a sailor without a sea, or a sea without a port. Without Jesus we are senselessly lost and without purpose.

But you are not without purpose, for you were created in God's holy image. Armed with this knowledge, your potential for completion knows few bounds.

On Being a Scout

A scout is someone who is willing to go ahead of the others, even if he doesn't know what lies before him. He is willing to risk the dangers of the unknown. He knows that he is equipped to handle the risks of the hour, so he is afraid only of not venturing forth.

A scout reports his findings to others, so that they too can pursue the battles to be fought and the treasures to be found. He loves learning and has a keen sense of adventure. No matter what his age, he has the heart and pride of a man.

In short, he is someone quite possibly like you.

What is in Store?

During Teleo Scouts, you will learn much about completion in Christ, but along the way you must keep this in mind—that all of the great things you will be learning and experiencing are for one purpose, and that is to know and experience Christ so that others may in turn also know Him.

Part of being complete or well-rounded means that you have a lot of experiences under your belt. Your scouting tenure will provide ample opportunity to do new things in new settings. In some cases you will sharpen already existing skills; in others, you will be like a boy cutting his teeth on grown-up food. But in all of this you will meet with success upon success.

One day you may be blasting clays out of the sky with a report heard the whole county over. On another you may be quietly finding your way north by northwest with nothing but a compass and a few provisions to aid you on your journey. Perhaps another day will find you in a spirited bout of competition, knocking your friend off his footing while he tries to knock you off yours. Another day might find you in a land you never knew was there. And to be sure, you will be helping others from time to time, for this is part of the Golden Rule.

You will be doing all of this with a band of like-minded young men. Together you will learn, work, play, plan, and create. Along the way, you will watch each others' backs, protecting one another like true brothers should.

How will you know when you are finally "complete?" One clue is that you will be a seasoned old man, far wiser than you are now, and you will in fact be so wise that you will think yourself foolish for knowing so little. Another thing—you will have finished the good race of life such that your feet will no longer touch the ground.

You can probably conclude that this won't all take place at once, but it's not too soon to start now!

Made for Fellowship

Some men pride themselves in becoming self-sufficient. Indeed, being able to take care of oneself is an admirable trait, but some men take it too far. Such men can be so proud that they rarely want to spend time with other people. These men may seem like they are sufficient, but in reality most of them live the lives of lonely hermits.

While God wants us to be self-sufficient in terms of taking care of our basic needs, He wants for us to be *interdependent* upon one another for deeper needs. These needs may include, but are not limited to, working, praying, learning, and playing. Sometimes it's great to be alone, but can you imagine trying to build a go-cart with no help? How about studying a difficult math subject with no one to help with instruction? Try shooting an elk in the mountains with no one to help drag it out. Or worse yet: imagine being in charge of a great tree fort with no one else to enjoy it!

To be sure, there will be times in your life when you will need to do these things alone, and it will be best that it be done this way. But such times will be the exception rather than the rule, for God has made us to be *communal*, meaning that He wants us to spend time with other people.

God has told us that by our love for one another will others know that we are His disciples. How, then, is this love to be manifested? God has told us how in His Holy Word! For starters, He wants us to know that His greatest commandment involves this very topic. A lawyer once asked Jesus this question:

> *"Teacher, which is the great commandment in the Law?"*

> *And He said to him, "'You shall love the Lord your God with all your heart, and with all your soul, and with all your mind.' This is the great and foremost commandment.*

> *The second is like it, 'You shall love your neighbor as yourself.' On these commandments depend the whole Law and the Prophets."*   *Matt. 22:36-40*

Loving God

Before all else, we are to love God with all of our being. Indeed, you will learn much about this during your scouting journey. You will learn about trusting God, having faith in His Holy Word, and revering His awesome safety and potential for wrath.

But in order to love God, you must know a few things, and these things must be driven into your mind and your heart so deeply that it would be impossible for anyone to steal these truths from you:

1. Know that you are a son of God. Because Jesus died for your sins, God has adopted you as a son, and you have rightful access to all that belongs to God because of this very fact (John 1:12, Rom.8:15-17).

2. You belong to God, and you are safe in His hands (Rom. 8:31-39).

3. You are made in God's image. God is a creator, a warrior, a conqueror, a lover, and a father. You too are made to be all these things (Gen. 1:26-28).

4. God has placed His Holy Spirit in you. The Holy Spirit is the Spirit of God, and He in fact resides in your body, which the Bible calls the "temple of God." You can have fellowship with God who dwells in you (John 7:37-39, John 14:15-17, John 16:7-13, Rom. 8:11).

5. God cares for you, listens to all you think and say, and takes delight in you.

So then, we are to love God according to who He is. Note that there is no one "right" way to do this. Simply love Him. Let Him know that all of your strength belongs to His service, that your personality is His for the shaping, and that your mind is His for the teaching. Take delight in Him as He delights in you. Do this however you care to, and know that by this He is greatly pleased.

Loving Others

Recall that the second part of Jesus' teaching is "You shall love your neighbor as yourself."

It is interesting that Jesus uses our love for ourselves as a sort of measuring stick for the manner in which we should love others. It is apparent that in order for us to properly love others, we must first have a proper love for ourselves.

Now if you are one of these boys who pouts and thinks that others are out to get him, then by all accounts you do not have a proper love for yourself. You may, in fact, love yourself too much or not at all. Simply stated, you must stop this kind of thinking at once, for you will never be able to properly love others. If this describes you, get over it and make it your life's goal to love God first and foremost forevermore. This will cure most of what you are lacking, and the rest will take care of itself.

So then, on to loving others. In your scouting experience, you will have ample opportunity to do so. And just as with loving God, there are a few things you will need to know:

1. The other young men in your scouting chapter are "brothers" in every sense of the word. They are brothers no less than the biological brothers you may have in your own, immediate family, for Jesus has made them so. Treat them accordingly (Matt. 23:8, Matt. 12:48-50).

2. You will do well to treat others "more highly than yourself." This is a sure way to guard against the temptation to be selfish.

3. It pleases God when you take pride in your fellow man. Be glad for his accomplishments, and feel free to "brag him up."

The above points are "principles of life," and you will do well to be governed by them during your scouting experience. Make them habits and standards to live by, and you will be blessed by your Maker while being a blessing to others.

Being Strong and Courageous

A Short Primer on Virtues

A virtue, as you may know, is an admirable trait usually associated with one's character. A person who is patient is said to be virtuous because he is so. Likewise, a person can be considered as having a virtue if he is kind. Creativity, thrift, and servitude are other examples of virtues. Virtues are fairly easy to spot in others because they are what make people truly attractive. Two of the most important virtues are strength and courage.

In the heart of every young man is a desire to be strong and courageous. This is self-evident, for what boy wants to be forever wimpy, or to become wimpy if he is not so already? The idea is laughable, if not deplorable, for there are few things sorrier looking than a boy needlessly stuck in his own jitters.

This, of course, does not describe you. But if you are honest, you have had to deal with the jitters at least once in a while. Rest assured you are normal. What is not normal, however, is being the kind of boy that is scared more often than not. God simply did not make you or any of His children to be this way.

Holy Strength

When we talk about being strong, it might surprise you that

what we are talking about has nothing to do with lifting rocks or curling barbells. If that is what you are after, then we applaud you. But don't neglect the more important kind of strength, and that is holy strength, the kind of inner strength that God has put into your reserve for whenever it is needed.

Barbell and dumbbell strength are nowhere near as useful as God's holy strength. For one thing, what good is the former when your body is sapped to the point of exhaustion? And barbell strength isn't any good in the middle of the night when a dream goes sour. Try lifting a downtrodden friend out of the blues with just your back; it simply doesn't work. Or try bench pressing a panel of accusers who want nothing more than to put you down. This won't work either; you might as well be whistling Dixie.

Can you imagine calling on your muscles when the experts announce that something awful is going to happen? What good will your muscles do when what you really need is an answered prayer? Rather, you need the strength of God to see you through. I would rather have an ounce of holy strength than to be able to curl three times my body weight.

"You Are Strong"

One of the most encouraging verses in the Bible is in John's first letter. He addresses this letter to his "children," who are those younger in the faith and have learned under his tutelage. Among other things, he instructs his readers so that they "may not sin," and he reminds them of the anointing of the Holy Spirit which abides in them (2:1, 2:27). And in doing so, he tells them something very pertinent and extremely encouraging, simple though it is. He tells them directly, "...I have written to you, young men, because you are strong, and the word of God abides in you, and you have overcome the evil one" (2:14).

If there is one verse worth taking to the bank, this is it. Let's hear it again, just for good measure: *"...I have written you... because you are strong...."*

Let me tell you something: John knew what he was talking about. He didn't have to size up every one of his readers to see if what he was saying was applicable to each one's specific condition. He knew that if his readers aligned themselves with Christ, then they were strong, whether they knew it or not. Before Jesus had died, John had eaten with, slept with, worked with, and learned from the Master. At one point he had even rested his head on Jesus' chest. He felt and heard the Lord's heartbeat, and he came to know that the Lord's holy strength would be ours for believing on His holy name.

After Jesus was crucified for our sins, John was an eyewitness to the risen Christ. He knew the power of the Holy Spirit in the believer, and so he could say with conviction that "you are strong."

John was one strong man himself. At the time of his writing, he was advanced in years, so he was at an age when a man's strength is really at its peak. Don't ever think that an old man is necessarily someone weak and feeble. If an elderly man is a Christian, he is in fact one of the strongest forces in all of nature. You would do well to revere such a man with a proper measure of awe.

I like the idea of an older man who knows way more than I do telling me something true as a matter of fact. If John says that you and I are strong, then let us all be the better for it by taking comfort in this truth. Let us all confidently walk knowing that what he says is so.

How Strong?

All of this talk about being strong may prompt you to wonder just how strong you really are. However, inner strength cannot be measured like push ups or bench pressing can. It can't be measured because no one has ever invented a scale that would work in this regard. Such a scale would be ridiculously bulky and would not be practical, for the springs and internal balances would instantly break under the simple strain of only one of your prayers.

Truthfully, neither you nor I know just how strong we really are. But it is probable that you are stronger than you think, for few of us realize the magnitude of heavenly power at our disposal. We wield a great and wonderful strength.

This much is sure: you are strong enough for what you and your loved ones need. Jesus said if you believe on His name, then you can move mountains (Matt 21:21). Because you will never literally need to move a mountain, then you can expect that Jesus meant this figuratively. Sometimes the challenges of life may seem like mountains to you, but you can move each one of these through faith in His name. That just about covers it all.

Weakness and Honesty

"But wait a minute," you say. "All this talk is fine and dandy, but I am pretty sure that I am not really as strong as you or the Bible says I am, and I don't think it is fair trying to fool myself otherwise."

Depending on your condition, this might be a fair objection. If you are simply trying to be honest in assessing yourself, then perhaps you are being humble in determining your capabilities. This is not a bad thing, and in fact can be the starting point for real strength in the making. But if you are merely being a sissy and have no real desire to be strong, then you are out to a lonely lunch, and not even Popeye's spinach will better your condition.

The Bible says, "Let the weak say, 'I am strong'" (Joel 3:10). How can this be? Because Jesus says that His power is made perfect in our weakness. If you are truly weak in one or more areas of your life, then it is fine to admit it. In fact, you can even glory in it as the great apostle Paul did, for then God can build you up like a potter builds a fine vessel (2 Cor 12:9-10). But what is not proper in admitting one's weakness, is to do so without envisioning a finer day when your weakness eventually becomes a strength.

All this business about strength arising from weakness might seem like a spin to simply suit our needs. Perhaps it does, but don't ever forget that God is in the business of spinning things to meet His ends. What we have encountered here is one of the Bible's finer paradoxes, whereby a seeming contradiction is really an eternal truth that makes perfect sense once you let God's Spirit reveal it to you. So then, let the weak say, "I am strong"!

Strength to Courage

It is one thing to have strength, but it is another thing to know what to do with it. The Bible lets us know that we are strong because of Christ who dwells in us, but it does not imply that we are instantly *courageous* as a result. In His wisdom, God has left the courageous part of the equation largely up to us. God would rather have us virtuous in this regard rather than programming us to be brave like so many robots. This is exciting news, for we get to play a part in advancing God's kingdom as a result of our desires and abilities. But make no mistake about it; it takes courage to do so.

Courage is the ability to capitalize on one's strength. It would not do well for a hunter to stand with loaded .300 Winchester magnum in hand, grizzly on the approach, if he were too skittish to aim and pull the trigger. Or imagine Neil Armstrong refusing at the last second to descend down the steps of the *Eagle* because he was afraid to touch the moon. Dale Earnhardt, Jr. would have never crossed the finish line, let alone come in first, if he were too chicken to put his foot on the gas pedal.

So then, you must become courageous if you are not already so. Without courage, you might as well join a support group for scaredy-cat men, the type who have difficulty mustering enough bravery to make it to the bathroom in the dark. God has made you to become courageous and in fact expects you to be so, for He has an adventure for you to live.

Courage—A Superior Virtue

Consider this: By exercising courage, any or all of the other virtues can be discovered, procured, and claimed as one's own. All a man needs to do is to desire a virtue, and then exercise the strength and courage to attain it. For example, if you want to become kind or patient because you are not, then you can be brave enough to become so. If true courage is being exercised and not some awful counterfeit, then any virtue can be captured and claimed as your own. This is a certainty. It may, of course, require an effort, but anything truly worth having is also worth the necessary battle.

The opposite is not true; no amount of nicety, wit, humor, or humility will ever be able to generate a single ounce of courage. Not even good luck can help in this manner. Courage, then, is one of the supreme virtues, right up there with faith, hope, and love.

Considering Heroes and Leaders

Think for a moment about one or more of your favorite heroes or leaders. What is it about these men that evokes admiration within you toward them? What virtues do they have that make you want to be like them in some way? Is it that they are simply "nice guys," the happy-go-lucky sort of chaps that sport stars on their foreheads for sitting still and being good? To be sure, the world could use a few more nice guys, but is merely being nice the stuff that heroes are made of?

Perhaps your heroes are nice enough, but you may be attracted more by their wit and cunning. These virtues are also valuable and are often in short supply, for too many men can't find a corner in a square room. Such men are said to not even have their wits about them. But wit and cunning are not ends of themselves; they are only minor virtues that never manifest their full potential without a greater good to govern them.

Think for a moment about some of the other, minor virtues: intelligence, self-control, and tolerance, just to name a few. You might even toss a good sense of humor in the mix. What good are any of these if a man is too cowardly to hone them for his use? I'll bet a dollar to a dime that the real stuff heroes are made of is two or three parts courage for every one part of the lesser virtues.

Becoming Courageous

So then, how can you become courageous? The good news is that you are probably off to a great start already, and you likely have a few good scars to prove it. The even better news is that courage is the kind of thing that grows like crazy. Once you get a little bit of it, the next thing you know you have more. You will even find at times that you have enough to give to those who lack. If you have ever had another man pass on to you some of his extra courage, then you know firsthand how this is possible.

Most young men can, with proper humility, recognize if they are courageous. If you are a reader who is having difficulty with this concept, then it could be that you are a bit too skittish and need a good dose of courage to get you out of your condition. Since we are in the business of good news, let's offer some more: It takes courage for a man to recognize his need for change and then to do something about it. Determine this very moment to be courageous from this day on, and ask the Lord for a special blessing of boldness. The severity of your condition will be instantly reduced, and you can in fact breathe easier. You will, of course, be tested in this regard, but I for one am placing my bet on you.

A Word of Caution

Before you are turned loose so that you can put all of this good stuff into practice, it is fitting that we part with a word of caution: Do not confuse courage with foolish pride. To be sure, you will experience your share of bruises in this life. But you can keep these to a minimum by assessing things moment-by-moment to see if the risks are worth the efforts. No amount of courage will make you fly if you do not already have some sort of wings, so always make certain that you are properly equipped for each dare that you take on.

A Proper Perspective

What is a young man like yourself to do with his strength and courage? Perhaps this is best answered by telling you what he should not do. For one thing it would be inappropriate for you to walk around like a proud rooster who thinks he is something special, when really all he amounts to is a stupid bird who takes his job too seriously. Another thing is that you want to be careful about whom you announce your strength to. It's probably all right showing off your accomplishments to your mother (it will do her even more good than it will you), but you might not want to crave audience from the neighbor lady. At best she will only think you are cute, and at worst you will irritate and maybe even frighten her.

Demonstrating your accomplishments to your friends can be a tricky thing. A good rule of thumb is to avoid this altogether if doing so is liable to make somebody jealous. Never mind if the other guy would be immature for being jealous; that is not the point. Just don't share your achievements with those that can't handle it. However, if you have some really cool friends that simply love to know what's new with you, then by all means show your stuff. Make sure when doing so that you exercise proper motives, and make certain you relish your friends' accomplishments as much as or more than they do yours.

The bottom line is this: It's okay to be strong and confident in the Lord and to know with certain confidence that you are so. Just remain humble in the entire principle of the matter.

TELEO SCOUTS
Completion In Christ

Social Skills

It is a matter of fact that we are often in the presence of other people. We are, then, in their *society*, and they are in ours. It stands to reason, therefore, that we would want to make the best of these situations by knowing how to conduct ourselves.

Your mother or father taught you long ago to make sure that you are presentable to others. You have at least been taught very basic manners like to say "please" and "thank you," to make an effort to match your clothes, and to cover your mouth and nose when you sneeze. In our society, these behaviors, if not conducted, become distractions to others. For good reasons or bad, we give cause for people to think poorly of us if we do not conduct ourselves with basic social skills.

Note that none of these behaviors, if neglected, is sinful in and of itself. Nowhere in the Bible does it specifically say that you should sit on the left side of the dinner table if you are left-handed, nor does it say that you should reply, "You're welcome" after somebody thanks you. Nevertheless, the benefits of considering our societal behaviors should not be dismissed. Nor is it a stretch to say that good, societal manners are the stuff from which virtues are made.

So then, what we hope to accomplish is to take our social skills to a higher plane, and we plan on doing so by offering a series of tips in this regard. We will not bore you with the basics; we assume that you know better than to block the sidewalk or to spit in public. If not, then we recommend that you enroll at once in a reputable school of etiquette to cure you of your shortcomings.

Rest assured, if you embrace and practice the following skills, you will become the better young man for it, and you will grow in favor with both God and other men.

Introductions

Along the way of life, you will often meet new people. Now observe the boy, who upon being introduced to one of his father's friends, immediately cowers and clings to his father's leg as though the other man were going to kidnap him. He neither offers a "hello" nor even looks the other man in the eye. When asked by his father to speak up, the boy feebly replies something so softly spoken that it is unintelligible.

What is wrong with this picture? Besides being an embarrassment to his father, the boy is being ridiculously selfish and is making the other man feel uncomfortable. We have all seen this picture.

It is important to drive home this point: that the other man in this scenario is made to feel uncomfortable. If that is what the boy wants to accomplish, then he might as well come right out and say, "You are a strange looking man and you scare me. I do not trust my father for showing you to me. You do not meet my standards for comfort as my Teddy bear does. My father coddles me, and so you should not expect any more than what you see from me. There is something very wrong with this moment, and I have determined that you are the cause."

This whole attitude in meeting new people is entirely unnecessary. As if you need convincing, none of your father's friends is going to kidnap you. Your father will teach you sufficiently to be on guard for weird behavior, but an introduction to someone new in the safe setting of your parents' presence is not the time to be on guard.

What to Do First

When meeting a new person, whether you are in the presence of your parents or not, simply follow the rules of proper conduct. For starters, smile, not forcefully, but naturally. Show the other person that you are glad to be in his or her presence. Also, make certain that you offer a sincere statement like, "Glad to meet you" or, "Hi, how are you?" You can be yourself in this regard, but no one will call you a copycat if you use a phrase that others successfully use. Just make sure you are sincere. Do not be in a hurry to get the matter over with. In fact, have fun with it, for you may be meeting a friend for life.

Eye Contact

Give people the courtesy of looking them in the eyes when they are talking to you. Of course, this is true for more than just introductions. In fact, provide adequate eye contact all the time. You need not worry about doing this too much; we have yet to see a young man make someone else think he was being hypnotized. Good eye contact makes people believe you are listening and that what they have to say is important.

The Handshake

In our culture, it is natural for men to shake hands with one another upon meeting. Even good friends will shake hands if they have not seen each other for a while. There is something to be silently said about a good handshake, as there is for a not-so-good handshake. A good handshake will be a firm one, at least as firm as the other person's, and perhaps perceptibly firmer, but only barely. Of course, this could theoretically result in a war of whose-is-the-firmer, but a handshake that got out of control in this regard is yet to be seen. By all means avoid offering a clammy, limpy handshake, the kind that makes the other guy wonder if you are all there.

If you have never done so already, ask your dad if you have a good handshake. He will give you the straight shot on this important matter.

Regardless of your age, take the initiative in shaking hands. An older gentleman will think it a kind and confident gesture if you offer your hand to his. He will feel like the next generation of young men is not so bad, after all. You will make him feel comfortable for making himself known, and he will be proud for knowing you.

There is some debate on whether or not it is appropriate for a young man to shake a lady's hand. It is probably best to consult with either your father or mother in this regard. At the bare minimum, you should at least say, "How do you do?" or some similar statement to your mother's friends or to other ladies you meet on the way. Certainly do not refuse to shake a lady's hand if she offers hers to you. But offering your hand to a lady can sometimes be an awkward thing. We counsel not to do it if it is possible that doing so will make the lady feel uncomfortable. Again, consult your parents.

Engaging in Conversation

If you are asked a question by someone, answer it in more than just a word or two. Remember the boy who clung to his father's leg after being introduced to someone? He is the same boy that answers in such a manner that we think he is either deaf, dumb, or both. If we are lucky, we might procure a short word in the way of an answer out of him. "Did you have a nice Christmas?" the boy is asked. After a delay of several seconds, the boy answers, "Good." Besides being grammatically incorrect, the answer is not satisfying, and so everyone is left thinking that something is quite wrong with the moment.

A good rule of thumb is to provide an answer that is at least as long as the question, and preferably longer. Give examples to back up what you are saying. Once the question is answered, be ready for more questions, or take the initiative and ask the same question back.

There is no better way to be a good conversationalist than to ask someone questions about himself.

A good idea is to watch and listen to someone who is good at all of this. There is absolutely nothing wrong with emulating what you see, and you will be the better for it.

Phone Skills

We use the phone a lot in our culture, and so you should know a few tips about this. For one, answer according to the preferred manner set forth by your parents. Do so confidently, as though you are an ambassador of your family (which you are). If the call is for someone other than yourself, then say, "Sure, I'll get him (or her) right away. Hold on please for just a moment." Be cheery in this regard in a manner that makes the caller feel as though he is being served.

While you are finding the person for whom the call was made, make sure that you fully cover the microphone. By all means avoid shouting, "Hey, Mom.......The phone is for you!" This may not sound bad on your end, but it does on the other.

If the party for whom the call is being made is not available, then say so, but do not do so in a mysterious manner. Probably the caller would like to either leave a message or know when to call back, so you can be helpful in this situation by asking if you can take a message. Again, be cheery in a spirit of servitude.

Your parents will help you fine tune these skills. These are actually easy skills to master, but too many people never do.

The Awfulness of Whining

If there is one thing that is intolerable in the heavens, it is whining. If you do not know what we mean, then you have either never heard whining or are immune to its effects for being party to it. We hope for your sake that it is the former. We fear for all if it is the latter.

There is no way we can beat around the bush on this matter. Whining is for selfish babies, not for men who align themselves with Christ. Whining does nothing to change the attitude of the matter, though it may serve to get one's way from time to time. If you are one who gets his way from whining, then shame on your parents or anyone else for allowing you to do this. But mostly shame on you. You need to repent of this dastardly behavior before it gets the best of you.

"But wait a minute," you state. "I don't whine. I only complain, and I do so in a nice voice." If this describes you, you have only proven that you are good at whining and know how to manipulate things to get your way. We are not saying that it is always wrong to complain, for there are true injustices that we sometimes must contend with.

A whine does not necessarily have to be audible. Rolling your eyes, shrugging your shoulders, or otherwise pouting are all non-verbal ways of accomplishing the same thing as whining. In fact, sometimes these are even worse.

If you feel you must voice a complaint or else you will bust, then you need to learn the fine art of making an appeal.

Making an Appeal

Making an appeal involves asking someone to reconsider a decision. We assure you, this is one of the most useful lessons you will have in terms of being a peacemaker, and it has all kinds of practical applications for life as well.

You do not want to ever get in the habit of always trying to get your way, so one rule is to not make appeals very often, especially when you are dealing with somebody who is in authority over you. Doing so will only frustrate the other person, and it will lessen your chances of being heard another day.

Perhaps the best way to make an appeal is simply to ask, "May I make an appeal?" While this may have a formal ring to it, I guarantee most of the mothers and fathers in the world would think it is just fine. Asking them this question indicates that you respect them, which is a great way to begin. You may also want to use a similar phrase instead, but just make sure you deliver it in a spirit of respect.

If the answer is a no, do not push the matter, especially if the other person is in authority over you. Simply reply with words to the effect, "All right, thank you for your consideration." You do not want to answer by pouting or demonstrating your disappointment with powerful body language; you will only irritate the other person by doing so.

Of course, if the answer is yes, then be ready to present your case. Consider beforehand all of the objections the other person may have, and be able to identify them. Doing so will let the other person know that you understand his or her concerns. This is called demonstrating *empathy*.

Then, in turn, offer answers for each of the problems associated with the other person's concerns. Be a problem solver, not a problem maker, and you will show others that you have everyone's best interest in mind. During the whole process, be as good of a listener as you are a speaker.

In the end, your appeal will either be granted or denied. If it is granted, then move forward in a spirit of appreciation. If denied, move forward in a spirit of respectful compliance.

Body Language

Sociologists have determined that over half of everything we really "say" to others is done non-verbally. This is called body language, and you should never dismiss the influence that your body has in telling others what you are thinking.

Always be aware of what your non-verbal cues may be saying to others. If you are tired and show it, you may run the risk of making the person think that he or she is boring. If you are frustrated, then squirming in your chair may tell the other person that he or she is causing you frustration. This may not be the effect you really want, so you should always be on guard for the messages you are sending with body language.

In regard to body language, there are few things more valuable than having a godly countenance. A countenance is a hard thing to describe, but essentially it is the overall expression shown on one's face. Have you ever seen someone who seemed to radiate joy, confidence, and peace all at the same time? If so, then you could probably tell these things from his or her countenance. Ask your parents if you have a godly countenance, and they will help you if necessary in this regard. The whole idea is to carry yourself in such a way so that others will find you a joy to be around.

Interrupting

The only time you should interrupt someone is if there is an impending terrorist attack or an immediate fire. Interrupting is rude, selfish, and altogether irritating. It is also usually unnecessary.

Of course, there are times when you want your voice heard, and by all accounts it will be too late if you don't speak up. There is a simple skill in this regard not used enough by young men, and that is to respectfully request an opportunity to interrupt. This can be done in a variety of ways, all of which will most likely grant you temporary audience. You can, for example, simply ask, "Excuse me, but may I interrupt?" Or you might request, "I beg your pardon, but may I ask a quick question?"

Be sensitive to those you are interrupting. If it becomes clear that your interruption is not a simple one after all, then gracefully offer to withdraw so as to pick up the matter at a later time. In all regards, you must not be demanding, not even a bit.

Part of interrupting properly is knowing that you will not always get your way. Be content for the moment with either acceptance or rejection.

Not all interruptions involve people that are already talking or engaging in quiet work. Perhaps you are playing a game with some friends, and you have an idea to make the game go better. You might simply state, "I've got an idea; mind if I share it?" In doing so, acknowledge what is already working well so as to save face with those who had the original ideas.

Once the interruption is over, thank the parties for allowing you to speak. You don't need to do anything fancy like take a bow, but do let them know you are appreciative.

Don't be like the boy who cried wolf who lost his credibility by announcing the need for an interruption too many times. Interrupt only sparingly so that when you do, your request will hold more weight.

It is essential that you realize that not all interruptions are committed verbally. Sometimes people interrupt without even knowing it because they lack empathy for the moment. For example, walking between two people who are engaged in conversation, crinkling paper when someone is speaking, or blocking someone's view are all interruptions. Go out of your way to avoid interrupting.

Being Loud

There seems to always be the boy who is louder than the others. We have even seen boys literally incapable of whispering, for their voices just can't make it happen. The loud boy really has no advantage, and in fact is at a disadvantage. He will seem boisterous when he doesn't intend to be, and others will fault him for it. Perhaps this type of boy has a hearing problem, or maybe he is simply oblivious to his condition. Are you one of these boys? If so, then make provisions for your remedy.

To be sure, there are a few prudish women and maybe even a few men who think it wrong for a young man to be loud from time to time. They are wrong, of course, but we must let them be so gracefully. However, we mustn't think that we can be loud whenever we want.

It probably goes without saying that being loud indoors is inappropriate well over ninety percent of the time. Our mothers told us this when we were young, and they were right. However, this does not mean that it is all right to be loud outdoors whenever the mood strikes us.

Be sensitive to others around you. If you are at a campsite, you owe it to others to demonstrate a peace appropriate to the setting. If you are at a football game, you do not need to think that you can scream your head off just because the guy five rows over has a bull horn. If you are standing in a public line, you may not want to laugh at the top of your lungs because you finally got the punch line to a joke told to you three days earlier.

Are we saying to be silent in these and all similar matters? Of course not. There is a season for everything, and this includes being loud. Joshua himself shouted during conquest (Josh. 6:15, 16). There will be adventures and battles with ensuing losses and victories that will give you no choice but to sound your own barbaric yawps, and no one should fault you for doing so.

Risky Humor

A good sense of humor is a tremendous commodity, for who doesn't appreciate being made to laugh? However, certain kinds of humor simply are not appropriate. Above all else, we must be careful about generating a laugh at the expense of others. Perhaps an example might be useful to drive home this point.

Suppose you were in the setting of some friends, one of whom is wearing long-legged pants that are obviously too short. It would probably not be a good idea to make the wisecrack, "Hey, Jim, are you waiting for a flood?"

In the above scenario, it should be assumed that the pants Jim is wearing for the day are the best ones he has on hand. For a number of reasons, it would be risky to make a wisecrack. For starters, Jim might not have too many choices in his dresser bureau, so it would not be proper to tease him for this apparent shortcoming. Also, Jim might not know that letting his socks show is unfashionable, so it would not be proper to correct him by making him look bad in front of the others.

Does this mean that you say or do nothing, and let Jim remain ignorant about being severely out of style? Actually, this might not be a bad option, for the good Lord is simply not too concerned about these types of things. But if you truly thought that Jim should know of his shortcoming, then you could do so in a non-offensive, safe way. There is a trick to this, and you will need wisdom in this regard.

It is vital that you guard other people's feelings when you are talking about non-eternal matters. Making risky comments about someone's bad breath, physical features, attempts at creativity, or apparent inabilities are simply out of line with mature conduct.

A word should be said about sarcastic humor. Some people have the gift of being sarcastic at just the right moments, and it comes off as being witty and non-offensive. If you don't know what we mean by this, then ask your parents or Scout leader for clarification. The point we want to make is that sarcastic humor is usually risky, and it is best that you avoid it unless you know for sure that it is safe.

Sometimes we hear a boy or girl state, "I was just kidding," in response to another person's objection to a previously made comment. You should never have to explain that you were "just kidding."

Bragging Rights

We need not cave in to the notion that it is wrong to be prideful of our accomplishments. Solomon himself said, "There is nothing better for a man than to eat and drink and tell himself that his labor is good. This also I have seen, that it is from the hand of God" (Eccl. 2:24). However, what is not good is boasting about it.

If we are to boast, we are to boast in the Lord (2 Cor. 10:13-18). The idea is to never forget that apart from Him we can do nothing.

However, the Bible tells us this: "Let another praise you, and not your own mouth; a stranger, and not your own lips" (Prov. 27:2). So then, accept praise from others, but be even more eager to give others praise.

In Teleo Scouts, we encourage you to brag up those in your group. Whenever you see something done well by someone else, declare it for all to see. You can do so even days later. Why not? Are you afraid of jealousy? We say that one of the best safeguards against jealousy is to recognize a strength in another and to celebrate it. By all means, do so!

This tip, like the others, is applicable all through life. You will do well to master it.

Appearance

We told you earlier that we would not bore you with the basics, and we will be careful not to do so now. But for the sake of others who must look at you, we want to make sure of a few things.

Simply stated, keep yourself looking good. There has been a long standing trend to be fashionable by being unkempt, and we resist this trend as being out of line with common decency. We are not saying that you should not have a wild side. But that which is wild is intended also to be tamed.

For goodness sake, comb your hair without having to be asked, and request a haircut when it gets too long. And watch what you wear; girls aren't the only ones who should be modest in their apparel. Wear what is decent, and not what shouts "look at me!"

We wish we did not have to address the current fad of altering your God-given appearance. Dying your hair, desiring tattoos, and piercing your body are radical expressions of one's inner man. If a boy has the need to be radical, he should be so in his faith and in his passion to help others before he entertains the fancy of altering his appearance.

Walk tall, not with arrogance, but also not with slumping

shoulders like you wish you were shorter than you are. You should have a bounce in your step, the kind that indicates that you are ready for action without being too much in a hurry.

The Sum of It All—The Golden Rule

If you can master the Golden Rule, then you will have mastered it all. The Golden Rule, as stated by Jesus, is this: "And just as you want people to treat you, treat them in the same way" (Luke 6:31).

Let others go first, and be eager to serve. "Can I get you something, sir?" should be one of the first things asked by you when your dad has company. "John, it's your turn to pick a game." "Bill, why don't you shoot first; show us how it's done." "Tommy, let me clean your gun for you, or let's do it together." "I'll be glad to" should be your reply when called into duty.

The ways to practice the Golden Rule are endless. Make it your life's mission to do so every step of the way.

Loving Righteousness and Hating Sin

You are going to get a bit of history and theology in this lesson. Theology, in case you didn't know, is the study of the nature of God as revealed in the Bible.

What is at stake here is our understanding of righteousness and sin. So the best way to get started is by defining these two things. Let's start with righteousness:

Righteousness

Righteousness is being right and just before God. God requires perfection in order to be right with Him. In order for you to become righteous, something first has to take place to declare that you are right and just. After this has taken place, you are said to be righteous, and you have attained righteousness.

The Bible tells us quite a few things about righteousness. Among other things, it tells us that "...there is none righteous, not even one" (Rom. 3:10). This means that no one is perfect, and so it seems that righteousness is not even possible.

The Bible also tells us that one man came who was perfect, and this was God's only Son, Jesus.

Sin

Sin is doing anything contrary to God's moral law. The Bible tells us that sin separates us from God. It lets us know that sin entered the world when the first man, Adam, did something other than what God directed him to do.

Sin really is not too difficult to understand. If God says something is wrong, then it is sinful to engage in that particular behavior.

The Bible tells us that "...all have sinned and fall short of the glory of God" (Rom. 3:23). Because no one is perfect, this has put the human race in a predicament. Remember, God requires perfection, and no one can enter heaven because all have sinned.

An Offering for Sin

In the days of old, God required that animals be sacrificed to make up for man's sin. These animals had to be as perfect as perfect could be, for God required nothing less. Without the shedding of these animals' blood, there was no forgiveness of sins (Heb. 9:22).

The Law of Moses

In addition to the sacrifices of animals, the Lord set up an impressive list of ordinances through the prophet Moses. These ordinances were called "The Law," and God's people had to obey the Law in order to be right with God. The trouble was, no one could do all that the Law required, and so everyone resorted to animal sacrifices to make up for their sins.

The whole thing was really rather taxing on everybody. There was a distance between God and His children that nobody could deny, and nobody could really be free from the oppressive constraints of the Law. On one hand the Law was a good thing, for it defined sin and let people know what was right and wrong. However, it was incredibly difficult to uphold and honor, and its affect prevented natural intimacy with God, the kind that was liberating and carefree.

A New Offering—This Time a Perfect One

In the fullness of time, God sent His Holy Son Jesus to be born from a virgin. When He grew to be a man, He ministered to God's people, showing everyone what God was really like. The amazing thing was that even though He was tempted in all ways like us, He was without sin (Heb. 4:15).

Jesus had come with the intention of offering Himself as a perfect sacrifice for our sins so that we would no longer have to be under the constraints of the Law, and so that we could have complete and direct access to God through His Holy Spirit who dwells in us. You see, before Jesus came, only kings and priests had direct access to God, and this had to be done through a cumbersome process.

Jesus' detractors and accusers did to Jesus what He would have done anyway; they put Him to death. They accused Him of sin which He did not commit, and then they crucified Him on a cross as the law of the day permitted. At any time Jesus could have saved Himself, but He used this opportunity to voluntarily lay His life down as a sacrifice for our sins.

A New Day

After three days, Jesus rose from the dead, for mere death could not keep a hold on Him. He appeared to many eyewitnesses and then ascended in glory to His Father in heaven.

A short while later, Jesus baptized the church with His Holy Spirit, providing this wonderful gift as He promised He would.

We have learned that the Holy Spirit is given to all believers, and that salvation is available to all who have faith in His name. In fact, the Holy Spirit now dwells in His believers, and He wants to fill us with His goodness so that we can advance His kingdom by telling others the good news about salvation in His name.

The gospel of John summarizes all of this into what is perhaps the most often quoted verse in the whole Bible: "For God so loved the world, that He gave His only begotten Son, that whoever believes in Him should not perish, but have eternal life" (John 3:16).

Righteousness and You

So then, you have been made righteous if you believe on Jesus' holy name. You need not be perfect, for perfection has already been provided for you from Jesus Himself, who was perfect.

This is good news, for you have direct access to God and no longer have to live in sin, which before was taking you on the low road to eternal death.

This, in summary, is what righteousness is all about. It's not really too hard to understand, but it can be wonderfully complex if ever you want to study it in depth.

What we want to instill in you, and this would be our highest aim, is a love for righteousness that would be greater than anything else imaginable. So imagine, if you will, your favorite food, your favorite hobby, or even your favorite person. Can you say, with all honesty, that you love righteousness more than any of these other things? If so, then we commend you, and we do not doubt you in the least, for we know full well that nothing compares to God's righteousness.

We commend you for loving righteousness, and we encourage you to do so all of the days of your life. Join us as we join you along the wonderful way.

The Final Word on Sin

Thanks be to God, that we no longer have to live in sin! When Jesus was crucified, He took the sins of the world upon His body. The Bible tells us that when we were baptized into Christ, we were buried with Him in the likeness of His death, so that our body of sin might be done away with and we would no longer be slaves to sin" (Rom. 6:6).

1 John 1:8 says that we deceive ourselves if we say that we have no sin. The next verse tells us that God will forgive us all our sins if we confess them, and that we are cleaned from all unrighteousness. 1 John 1:10 says that we make God a liar if we say we have not sinned, and so we must acknowledge that we have had to contend with sin.

In 1 John 2:1, we find why all of this was written: "My little children, I am writing these things to you that you may not sin. And if anyone sins, we have an Advocate with the Father, Jesus Christ the righteous.

So then, we no longer have to live in sin. John tells us further: "And you know that He appeared in order to take away sins; and in Him there is no sin. No one who abides in Him sins; no one who sins has seen Him…No one who is born of God practices sin, because His seed abides in him; and he cannot sin, because he is born of God" (1 John 3:5-6, 9). Your body of sin was put to death, and so let this be the final word on the matter.

Of course, sin may lurk at your door, but the Bible tells us that "No temptation has overtaken you but such as is common to man; and God is faithful, who will not allow you to be tempted beyond what you are able, but with the temptation will provide the way of escape also, that you may be able to endure it" (1 Cor. 10:13).

Hating Sin

It is enough to say that sin is to be hated. It will, to be sure, show its ugly head. But returning to it is like a dog returning to its vomit. There is nothing that can be said that will bring glory to this topic.

Let us offer some strong advice in the way of hating sin. You will inevitably hear somebody make a crass joke which attempts to glorify sin. Or you may be exposed to something which attempts to celebrate it. For sure you will see brutes disguised as decent people engage in it.

In all of these situations, neither laugh nor commend the sinners' behaviors. Don't even crack a smile so as to give applause to their efforts. Simply remain unmoved, and let them know you do not approve. Do so, however, in a manner which leads them to the Better Way.

It is a sure thing that you will meet more sinners than saints during the course of your life. In our admonishment for you to hate sin, we implore you to never wish ill upon a sinner or consider yourself more privileged than he. On the contrary, extend your love toward such a person as you would extend your arms to a drowning man. Can you be friends with those who do not understand righteousness? Of course you can; Jesus was a friend and more to sinners, and it shall be your privilege to do likewise!

The Foundation for All Else

The things you have learned in this short lesson are foundational for everything else that you will learn. Keep them on the forefront of your mind. Know that good and evil are realities in this world, and that you can forever stand on the side of good. Know that true goodness comes from Christ alone, and the war of righteousness versus sin has been won by Him. Rejoice in this wonderful truth, and may all that you learn henceforth be built upon this solid foundation!

Honoring Your Parents

The Commandment with a Promise

The Bible tells us: "Children, obey your parents in the Lord, for this is right. Honor your father and your mother (which is the first commandment with a promise), that it may be well with you, and that you may live long on the earth" (Eph. 6:1-3).

Make no mistake about it. God wants you to obey and honor your parents. In this lesson, we will give you some insight and tips as to how to do this effectively.

The Clingy Boy

In our lesson entitled "Social Skills," we talked about the boy who sheepishly clung to his father's leg while being introduced to someone. As you recall, he provided an effective albeit pathetic display of selfish cowardice. Well, he is back by popular demand for the purposes of this lesson. But we warn you, even though he is a bit older, he hasn't grown up much:

The boy is now "helping" his mother with her weekly shopping. The trouble, however, is that he is more harm than help.

"Why do I have to help you with the shopping, Mom?" he

complains, as his mother puts back the potato chips that he tried to sneak into the cart.

"Now Klinger, don't sass me. You know Father would not approve of your attitude."

"I'm not sassing, and Pops wouldn't mind if we bought some potato chips. Can't we at least have some M & M's or at least some Doritos or Cheese Puffs for a snack?"

"You are sassing. Now go over to aisle eight and get me some pork rinds. Get just one bag. Now hurry, because I've got a few more items for you to get."

"I'm hurrying," says the boy, but it is clear that he is not.

Stop the Film

Now, let's stop this film for a minute. What do you think of little Klinger so far? Do you think he is just a bit misdirected, but otherwise cute? Do you side with him because shopping with one's mom is not your idea of fun? Or do you consider him, simply enough, a brat?

Let's all talk to Klinger directly. Perhaps he won't be too aloof:

Back to the Action

"Excuse us," we say. "Do you know where we can find the pork rinds?" Our friend is a bit startled but composes himself fairly well.

"Umm, yeah. They're right there," he says, pointing to the lower shelf, while holding yet another bag of potato chips.

"Thank you," we reply. "Do you mind if we make an

observation? It appeared that you were talking back to your mother a moment ago."

"I was not talking back. I was only letting her know that we need better snacks," he says.

"Oh, we see. By the way, we are from Teleo Scouts. What is your name?"

"Klinger," he responds, a bit on guard as perhaps he should be.

"Oh, that's an unusual name. Is it a nickname?"

"Yeah, one of my dad's friends started it."

"Oh, we see. Hey, I thought your mother wanted you to get some pork rinds. Why are you clinging to those potato chips instead?"

"Umm, I dunno. I guess I made a mistake," he replies, reluctantly trading in the potato chips for pork rinds.

Back to the Present

Okay, let's take ourselves out of the picture. What can we conclude about Klinger?

We can tell one thing right off the bat: Klinger does not honor his parents. This much is sure, for the Bible says that what comes out of our mouths comes from our hearts. He is a sassy boy, no doubt about it.

We should not be too surprised that Klinger is also selfish, for selfishness and sassiness go hand-in-hand. He wants his way, not his parents'. We happen to know that his mother fills the kitchen with all kinds of great snacks. But he is too much into himself to even realize it.

He also tries to pit his mother against his father by declaring that his father would not like his mother's decision. His attitude was such that he was trying to create division.

Furthermore, he is a pouter. We could tell this by the fact that he did not hustle to aisle eight like his mother requested. If he wasn't pouting, you sure couldn't tell it.

Moreover, this boy is prone to going on the defensive. Note that instead of owning up to the fact that he was talking back to his mother, he defended himself. His explanation, however, only further proved him to be wrong.

To top it all off, Klinger is a liar. You and I know full well that he was holding on to the potato chips so that he could somehow con his mother into buying them, just like he did earlier. We caught him red handed, but he tried to cover himself up.

This poor boy is a piece of work. Unfortunately, he is representative of too many others like him. You will do well to do the opposite of all that he does. Maybe you will get to meet Klinger in real life someday. Hopefully he will have grown up a bit by then. But in the meantime, let us hope we can learn from his actions so that we can know what it means to honor our parents.

Pressing "Pause"

To be sure, there will be times when you will meet real people that remind you somewhat of our poor friend, Klinger. You will, no doubt, observe boys and girls, and even adults who make him look angelic by comparison. On the opposite side of the coin, you will meet others who do a commendable job of conducting themselves toward their parents.

In all of these cases, we advise you from time to time to press "pause" and consider what you are observing. In other words, learn from what you see and from what you hear. Identify the fool, the brat, the punk, and the idiot so that you can determine why he is so.

Likewise, if you see a young man who is respectable toward his parents and others, determine what makes him this way. Once these observations have been made, you will have a wealth of knowledge as to how to conduct yourself.

The Blame Game

It is possible that Klinger may believe that his parents are to blame for his condition. Truth be told, they may be to blame, at least in part. You may have wondered why his mother let him come shopping in the first place, or why she let him get away with sassing. You may have even wondered why she didn't take him out to the car to give him a thrashing, or why she didn't at least ground him for a few months. In short, you may suspect that she was not in complete control.

Your observations may be accurate, but let's make something clear: This lesson is not about parenting; it is about becoming more complete in Christ by honoring our parents. It is sufficient to say that none of our parents is perfect. We do not honor them because of how perfect or imperfect they are. We honor them because it is right to do so.

The Best Source for Knowledge

The best way of learning how to conduct yourself toward your parents is to simply listen to them. Ever since you were birthed into this world, they have been parenting you, and God has made them stewards over you. In many ways, they know you better than you know yourself. All along the way, they have let you know what pleases them and what does not.

What do you think? Are your parents pleased with the degree of honor you give them? How do you rate yourself? In what ways can you improve?

Would you like to provide your parents with an instant blessing? Ask them, even today, how they rate you in regard to the honor you afford them. Ask in a spirit of humility, in a manner that lets them know that you really want to be a blessing to them. Your act of asking alone will bless them, and it may lead to a wonderful conversation that could enhance both of your lives.

Practical Tips

If you are like us, then you like straightforward tips that don't leave you guessing. This lesson would not be complete without a few. We promise: these tips are universally accepted by all parents; not one parent would object to anything on this list. Pick a few out, and if you haven't already put them into practice, do so. You will be the surprise and delight of your parents!

First Time Obedience

You may consider yourself pretty good at obeying. But do you do so at once, without delay, or do you try to get a few words in to somehow get your way? If it is the latter, then you will do well to quicken your response time.

Obey your parents right away; don't make them repeat themselves.

Mom vs. Dad

Do you ever tell one of your parents that the other parent has a different take on a matter? If so, do you do so primarily to get your own way? If this is the case, it should be apparent that you have ill-motives. You should feel badly enough without us scolding you.

There will be times when it is appropriate to let one parent know that the other thinks differently. Do so if you know for certain that both parents will be glad you provided this information.

Do you ever go to one parent with a request because you suspect the other parent will not answer as favorably as the other? This is an age old trick. Sometimes this might be appropriate, but it is definitely never appropriate if you know that the other parent who is left in the dark would be upset if he or she knew what you were up to.

Chores

Can we really say anything here that you don't already know as it applies to chores? Probably not, but we will try:

Perform each and every chore completely and thoroughly. When done, use this wonderful phrase, which is music to any parent's ears: "I'm finished with my work. Is there anything else I can do?"

Help your siblings finish their chores from time to time, even often.

Have a great attitude when doing chores. Work can be a terrific blessing, and your parents will love it if they see that you work with a merry heart.

Bedtime

Bedtime can be a tense time at many households. Really, it should be a rather peaceful time. Do your part to make it peaceful by going to bed on time, without being told.

Now, once you are in bed, fulfill the spirit of your parents' wishes, and not just the letter of it. For example, if what your parents mean by being to bed on time includes lights out, then have lights out. But also note that they probably mean that you should have the radio off as well. If you are being sneaky, then you are being out of line.

Sibling Fellowship

Your brothers and/or your sisters are sometimes called your siblings. If you have brothers or sisters, can you say with all honesty that they are your best friends? If not, would you like them to be? We hope so, for this would bless your parents beyond measure, more than all of the other tips in this lesson put together.

Considering your siblings as your best friends will not only bless your parents; you will be blessed as well. And more importantly, God will be blessed. Just as one day you will be a father and will want to see your children live in loving harmony, so does God want you to love your siblings.

So here's our tip: From time to time, even often, think of your siblings and pray for them and for yourself. Ask God to knit your hearts together. Ask God to show you how to be the best brother that you can be to your siblings. Let your parents and your siblings know that this is your heart's intent, and then let God answer your prayers. There may be no greater prayer that God wants to answer. But understand that you must do your part, and that is to be the kind of brother that will make God, your parents, and your siblings proud.

There's more to this tip: Are you a big brother to one or more of your siblings? If so, then you have an incredible obligation and privilege to lead them toward right living. It may not be too much of a stretch to say that your parents can't do this alone; they literally need you to help raise the younger ones in your family. They need you to teach your younger siblings all kinds of important things, and in many ways you are the most qualified to do so. Take pride in this wonderful fact. Your little brothers or little sisters need you to lead by example the way toward good and important things, and your part in their lives will make both them and you richer for it.

Are you a little brother to an older sibling? If so, then good! You have the great privilege of learning to be a follower, and in doing so you will be teaching yourself to one day lead. We implore and direct you to let your older siblings lead the way, especially if they are your older brothers. Never try to take away their birthright from them. If they are older than you, then be proud of them for it. You may think that your older siblings have perfect and rosy lives; if so, you are wrong in your assessment. Regardless, you should defer to them in nearly everything. Serve them as you would your father. Let them know you admire them when they give you reason to do so. Brag them up and be proud of them.

We once witnessed a poor boy who wanted his older brother's position. He wanted all of his brother's privileges; he wanted his brother's income, his curfew, and even his belongings. The poor lad made all kinds of trouble for everyone involved. We predicted he would turn out to be a sassy boy who liked nothing better than to sulk. Unfortunately, we were correct. We hope this boy will realize where he went wrong and will repent of his selfish ways.

If you are a younger brother and are in any way concerned that you will be left behind by letting your older brother lead, then take ironic comfort that you were behind to begin with, and you are out of line by wanting to be ahead. But take comfort also that by following, you will be living a life that will give your older brothers and sisters cause for being proud, and you can be sure that they will be learning all kinds of things from you as well.

Your Friends

We implore you to keep good company in regard to your friends. More times than not, a man's choice of friends is a reflection of his own values. You will do well to hang around the kind of friends that will make your parents proud. Choose friends that will lift you up and encourage you, rather than those that will tempt you to compromise your convictions.

Are we saying that you must always avoid non-Christians? By no means! On the contrary, Jesus Himself extended friendship to those who did not know Him. If you truly are a lover of people, as Jesus is, then you will want to engage in conversation and spend time with those who do not know Him. We encourage you to do so. But your intent is to lift the lost one up to a higher place, not be party to his folly.

Proverbs 28:7 says, "He who walks with wise men will be wise, But the companion of fools will suffer harm." This verse pretty much speaks for itself. If the company you keep is foolish, you will eventually pay a price. Honor your parents' direction in this regard.

Be a Light

We recall a bit of encouragement that a wise man once gave us. After a couple of decades or so of raising several children, he concluded that one of the best ways to show others the love and power of Christ was for them to see the love and power at work within the family. We have seen that his observations are true.

If you want to be part of letting others know the love of God, then be a good witness to them. Jesus said, "So let your light shine before men, that they may see your good works and glorify your Father who is in heaven." He also said, "By this will all men know that you are my disciples, that you have love for one another."

You will be surprisingly refreshed by the compliments your family will receive when others see that you love God and that you love your parents and siblings. The world is full of families that do not love God nor one another, and by showing your love you will be showing God.

When others see the love that your family has for one another, you will have additional opportunities to share your faith. Be proud to tell others of your family's love for one another and that you experience the power of Christ's unity, and encourage them to do likewise.

A Legacy

A legacy is something handed down from somebody to those who come after him. By now you know several ways in which you can honor your parents, and in doing so you will be solidifying a legacy which you can pass down to your children. You will also be securing others' ability to come to Christ, for you will be light to them to show the way.

So then, let honor toward parents have its way!

Treating Ladies Properly

If you are in Teleo Scouts, then by default you are in your teens or are very close to being so. And if you are in your teens, then you are beginning to see girls in new and different ways.

You have probably noticed long ago that girls are different than boys in more ways than just their body parts. They are different on a number of fronts. They are so different, in fact, that they can be almost impossible to figure out without learning from observant men who have gone before you. This topic needs special treatment, for girls should be specially treated.

It might be useful to note that not all men have been observant in figuring out the female gender. From ancient days to the present, many men have ruined their marriages, their families, and themselves because they never took the time to observe and learn how to treat ladies properly.

What Does the Bible Tell Us?

Indeed, much has been written and discussed by so-called experts in regard to the differences between men and women. Some of these "experts" even claim to be Christian. Regardless of what has been previously declared, we must be certain that purported truths have a biblical foundation before we consider their usefulness.

As with all things, if the Bible says something is so, then it is so. If worldly philosophies and ideas emerge which add to or contradict what the Bible says, then we can categorize such ideas as being false. Falsehood is always harmful and is best disposed of in the garbage as soon as it is found.

Let's move on to identifying what the Bible says about ladies and how we should treat them:

In God's Image

You have already learned that like the first man, Adam, you are made in God's image. But did you know that women are also made in the image of God? This fact is clear, for the Bible tells us, "And God created man in His own image, in the image of God He created him; male *and female* He created them" (Gen. 1:27, emphasis added).

There is an old nursery rhyme that says that girls are made of "sugar and spice and everything nice." If there is any truth to this statement, then we should be able to see these same qualities in God. There is indeed a sweetness to our Lord that will one day be evident to you if you have not already tasted it. And certainly God is full of every good spice under the heavens, for He seasons His creation for our good pleasure and betterment. And He is, to be sure, the author of all that is nice.

Jesus referred to God as our "father" dozens of times, and so it may seem easy for us to visualize God as a father figure. But God has maternal qualities as well; it is He who nurtures us as children, raising us from infancy to maturity. Note the imagery that Jesus used when He agonized over the holy city, "O Jerusalem, Jerusalem, who kills the prophets and stones those who are sent to her! How often I wanted to gather your children together, *the way a hen gathers her chicks under her wings*, and you were unwilling" (Matt. 23:37, emphasis added).

So then, a godly lady is just as much like God as is a godly man, and it is essential that you understand this first before trying to understand anything more about the matter. Many men have failed to recognize this crucial fact.

Truth vs. Worldly Equality

Sometimes it is useful to identify what is true by first identifying what is not true. Indeed, there are a number of emerging falsehoods regarding this topic. We will discuss one of the more significant ones here.

There is the idea, embraced by many, that men and women are equal in all regards. These people have even fought to have an amendment added to the U.S. Constitution that would make this ridiculous idea into law. The Bible does recognize that "… there is neither male nor female; for you are all one in Christ Jesus" (Gal. 3:28). But in context this simply refers to the fact that men and women are equal as belonging to Christ.

Let's set the record straight: Men and women are not equal in all regards. In many ways, in fact, women are superior to men. Ask any man who truly loves his wife if she has power and influence over him that is greater than his over hers, and you will find this to be so. A godly lady is arguably the most beautiful and potent force in all of creation. On the flip side, men have certain strengths that women do not.

You should know that there are also those who believe that men are actually inferior to women. Along with this idea is the notion that women can get along fine without men, and that most men have it out to oppress and take advantage of women. These types of people are called *feminists*, and the worldly philosophy they embrace is called *feminism*. Most of these people are unfortunate women who simply have an axe to grind, and they would like to use men as their sharpening stones if not their actual chopping blocks. Quite likely these women were at one time emotionally wounded by abusers disguised as men, and so we should feel sorry for them, for they simply do not have the truth of God's Holy Word.

In the meantime, do not let the ideas of feminism have a bad influence on you. Feminists would like nothing better than to make you into a sissy by getting you to think that men are nothing more than unnecessary brutes. Pay no attention to these foolish people and their ungodly ideas.

On Being a Gentleman

In 1 Pet. 3:7, Peter tells husbands to "...live with your wives in an understanding way, as with a weaker vessel, since she is a woman; and grant her honor...." Let's take note of the part about treating women "as with a weaker vessel."

There is an important point to be made here, and that is that Peter never says that women actually are weaker vessels. He simply says to treat them as though they were. There is a fine difference between the two, and many men never catch this important detail.

Another thing: In biblical times, a "weaker vessel" often referred to pottery that was specially made, so much so that it took a fine artist or potter to craft it. The final product was one that was strong enough to use, but delicate enough to be called beautiful. It may have been something similar to what we call fine china. This "weaker vessel" was, in fact, far more valuable than the more common pottery. So in context, Paul was placing tremendous value on women in referring to them in this manner.

There is certainly nothing that indicates that women suddenly become weaker once they are married. So then, if married men are to treat their wives as though they were the weaker vessel, then it is appropriate that unmarried men treat unmarried ladies likewise.

Simply stated, a man should be a gentleman toward a lady. And for those who don't already know, a gentleman is a man who is gentle.

Ladies First...

For starters, let ladies be first (and this includes even very young ladies). They should be let in the door first, seated first, and served first. In between all of this, you should open the door for them, take their coats, and otherwise offer them comfort.

Why are we doing all of this? Is it because they are weaker? Heavens no, for we have already learned that this is not necessarily so. Is it because we are trying to impress them? Our answer is again no, for then we would be drawing attention to ourselves. Rather, we are simply giving them their due honor. It is not a stretch to say that they deserve to be treated in a manner which approaches royalty, for ladies are created to be queens as much as you are to be a king (Rev. 1:6).

Of course, you can go overboard on all of this to the point where you can look awkward. If you are opening a door for a lady, as you should, you do not have to bow or say something British and old-fashion sounding like, "After you, my lady." If there is any question on the lady's face as to intent, then by all means you should simply say, "After you," but anything beyond this is overkill. Your parents may want you to address a lady older than you by "Ma'am," and of course you should do so if this is the case.

If ever you are serving food in mixed company, by all means serve the ladies first, including, of course, your mother and sisters.

If you are done with your chores and have extra time to help someone else out, consider helping a sister before a brother. In fact, if your sister, mother, or one of their friends needs help, offer assistance as soon as you can.

By now you should be getting the idea. Probably you are already off to a good start, and if so, then you can use what we have discussed here to hone your already existing skills.

From Cooties to Beauty

Not too many years ago, you may have seen girls in a different light than you do now. It may have been that you felt as though they had germs or "cooties" because they were so different than you. You may have wanted to avoid them for the better things in life like catching frogs, making mud, or chopping down trees.

In recent times, however, you may have started to think of girls a bit differently. If you haven't as of yet, you will, and rest assured, you are very, very normal.

You may have noticed, quite frankly, that they have a form and beauty that you did not previously recognize. We affectionately call this transition "from cooties to beauty."

You will need some guidance in making this transition, for without it, you would be like a running back carrying a greased football; you would be sure to fumble the moment you got hit.

Attraction

Nature declares it and the Bible affirms it: A woman can be a beautiful thing. Now we should take a minute and consider this fact. What is it about a woman that can make her attractive? For one thing, she might be physically attractive. This is possibly the first thing we might notice, for we can tend to see with our eyes before we see with our hearts.

In a chapter called "To Young Men," T.L. Haines wrote,

"Gaze not on beauty too much, lest it blast thee; nor too long, lest it blind thee; nor too near, lest it burn thee: if thou like it, it deceives thee; if thou love it, it disturbs thee; if thou lust after it, it destroys thee; if virtue accompany it, it is the heart's paradise…."

Indeed, beauty is there for the seeing, but it must be perceived and appreciated appropriately.

Counterfeit Beauty

Imagine a woman who is attractive only in appearance. This particular woman, though she may be considered "pretty" by some, nonetheless does not honor God's Holy Word. She either knows nothing about our good Lord, or she has flat out rejected Him after knowing better. Perhaps she is a blatant rebel, a liar, a lost and illiterate loner who longs for attention and will do anything to get it. Or perhaps she is not quite so bad, having a redeeming quality or two; she may be a thief but is a truthful thief, or a liar but a gentle one in being so. Any way you cut it, however, she does not love God, and all the beauty in the world cannot make up for this glaring deficiency.

Can we not declare that such a woman is, in fact, ugly to the core and not beautiful at all? Can we not say, as the heavens do, that she is as "filthy rags" as is anyone who does not honor and love the Lord? Can we not say, with certainty, that we should run from her advances as we would run from a foreign terrorist?

Make no mistake about it; women like the one we have described have the potential to be attracted to any man, including ones who align themselves with Christ. We tell you now that such a woman is an ugly one, and at this point we will not even give her the courtesy of calling her a lady. If you will but see with your heart, we will not have to convince you much, for you will determine for yourself that we are being kind when we say she is ugly.

True Beauty

If you love God, as we trust that you do, we will not have to describe true beauty to you. It will, for certain, be self evident. Nevertheless, we will declare what your heart already knows, that true beauty will have nothing whatsoever to do with physical beauty and everything to do with inner beauty.

True beauty in a lady can be seen in her countenance. It is the product of the fruit of the Holy Spirit: love, joy, peace, patience, kindness, gentleness, and self-control (Gal. 5:22-23). Possibly included in this will be a measure of wit and good humor. You will know it when you see it. Someday, you will take a wife to be your own, and you will do well to align yourself with a woman who bears such fruit.

In Her Presence

To be sure, you will be in the presence of ladies who have undeniable, inward beauty. How should you behave in such an occurrence? Let us assure you, you need not fumble when this happens. Simply enjoy the occasion and recognize that you are being graced by one of God's many handiworks.

Treat such a lady just as you would your own sister. You might, in fact, appreciate her in some ways differently than your sister, and this is just fine. However, love her only as a sister, and nothing more. For when we say "nothing more," we are, in fact, declaring the highest measure.

Beauty, Marriage, and the High Duty Between Now and Then

You have the high duty of honoring all ladies, and this includes honoring them in thought and in deed. You are at a wonderful point in your life whereby the Lord is preparing you for marriage, and you should know a thing or two to prepare for high duty as it pertains to the entire matter of treating ladies appropriately.

We need to get right to the point. In marriage, there is given by God a gift of sensuality, whereby a man can look upon the physical beauty of his wife without constraint. He will not have to concern himself with whether or not he is gazing upon her beauty too much, for it will be impossible for him to do so.

However, you are not yet married, though one day you may be. In the meantime, your body may respond as though it is married, and rest assured, you are normal. You will experience changes in your body appropriate to becoming a man. Your body will be preparing itself for marriage, and because your body does not know when you will get married, it is preparing itself in advance. Your parents and your scout leader will talk to you more about this, giving you sufficient details and guidance to lead you into manhood.

We will take the opportunity here to offer you at least a couple of challenges and words of encouragement. For starters, we challenge you to purpose from this day forward that the only lady besides your mother, grandmother, or aunt that you will kiss will be your wife, and that you will wait until your wedding day to give her this kiss. The Bible tells us that it is not good for a man to touch a woman unless they are married (1 Cor. 1:7). We have seen that even some Christians disregard this wonderful, biblical truth, but you will do well to heed its wisdom. Besides, there will be a rich reward that is worth the wait.

Also, you must know that it is morally wrong to look at beauty as though it were something for you to possess. There are brutes disguised as men who think it is okay to look upon a woman's body, even though they are not married to her. These men want to possess what is not theirs, and they will suffer eternity away from God if they do not repent of their foolish, selfish, and insecure ways.

Possession of women outside of marriage is fueled by base and fleshly desires, including lust, deception, and power. It is sinful to think in such a manner. Remember, you are to treat ladies in both thought and deed as though they were your sister. Anything more than this is utterly sinful.

Here's the encouragement: This whole matter of treating ladies properly is not all that difficult if you keep the simple truths that you know dear to you. If you purpose to see with your heart and not just your eyes, most of what is involved with treating ladies appropriately will come naturally. Also, know that many, many men have gone before you who have not failed in this manner—men who, though not perfect, have purposed and learned to respect inner beauty rather than outer beauty. You are equipped as they are, with the Spirit of God who indwells you.

Flirting

Do not give a lady reason to believe she is something special, not unless you have your parents' permission, are preparing for marriage, and you have thought the whole matter out. These kinds of emotions are part of growing up, and you will learn more about them in the lesson we call "Made for Marriage."

In the meantime, do not show off to a lady. Nor should you make a lady feel that you like her more than a sister. You should simply not try to get a lady's attention with the motive of getting her to like you. Doing so is called "flirting," and it is, in fact, a sin. Besides, what would you do with her attention once you got it? Brag to the neighbors about it? Announce to your parent that you're ready to get married?

You learned earlier that as a young man, you wield a great and wonderful strength. If you are not careful, you could wield your strength and power in such a manner as to cause a young lady to be emotionally attracted to you. While this might be the goal of some boys, it should not be one of yours. You could make a young girl vulnerable to emotional pain if she gives part of her heart to you only to find later that you do not want it.

The kind of attention we are describing is the kind that should be reserved for marriage. It is best to avoid giving or receiving this kind of attraction until you are ready to give a lady your heart, and she is ready to give you hers, with no turning back.

If ever your affection goes beyond natural attraction, talk to your parents and your scout leader about it. It may be that something needs to be addressed. They can provide the guidance you need.

Pride and Attraction

You will probably experience a time when a lady finds you attractive, and you may feel a sense of pride welling up within you as a result. Watch out! While this pride can be a natural and proper thing, it can also be destructive.

We are not telling you to not feel special if a lady thinks you are special. What we are saying is not to go looking for this to happen. For goodness' sake do not let your sense of worth depend on it. If you feel you are "one up" on a friend or a brother because some gal finds you attractive and he has no such luck, then you can be sure that pride is beginning to fester, and you had best pluck the thorn of pride out before you become infected.

Are you the kind of young man who thinks he is something special because you are good looking? If so, then we fear for you. You will be better off by either repenting or asking the Lord to color you blue if this is what it will take to cure you. Have you seen a proud boy who thinks he is good looking? We ask you to determine for yourself: does not such a boy appear conceited, foolish, and downright silly? You would do well to place a low value on the concept of good looks.

Made for Sisterhood

To be sure, you will meet many girls who are not godly, and so you might wonder how you should treat them. We encourage you to treat them as sisters-in-the-making, for God wants each and all of these ladies to one day know Him as their Lord. So then, treat them as you would any non-believer, with the recognition and respect of their awesome potential for greatness under the loving Lordship of our Savior.

In Closing

How might we summarize the proper treatment of ladies? If you can respect a godly lady as a sister in the Lord and recognize her God-given qualities, you will have summed up the matter on your own.

Does this mean that you will be fond of all the girls that come your way? By no means do we suggest this, for we know that some girls will seem so odd to you that you will find it difficult to even be around them. One girl you meet may think that hunting is cruel, or another might think that football is a stupid sport. Yet another girl may like nothing better than to gossip, and another might think she is the Queen. In such circumstances we counsel you to simply do your duty to be a gentleman while around them, but nothing is required beyond this.

Will the counsel we have given you today be all you will ever need to understand ladies? Ha! Not on your life, for men have tried for centuries to figure out all the peculiarities of women, and some have driven themselves half crazy in their attempts. Indeed, there is strangeness inherent in the opposite gender, but it is a wonderful strangeness. Much of it is too wonderful for words, and we could not fully explain it if we had all the paper and ink in the world!

Being a Great Worker

It is a sure statement that men were made to work. Some men who have wanted an excuse to be lazy have denied this, but they are quite wrong. There are nearly as many arguments against work as there are lazy men. One argument is that the government should provide our needs. Another argument is that work is bad for you. Yet another claims that work is boring. There is even the argument that work is a burdensome thing, part of the great curse upon mankind for Adam and Eve's sin, and that life on earth at one time was only blissful relaxation, void of any need to work. All of these arguments are lazy to the core, lazier even than the men who speak them, for none of them has the strength to stand up to even ten seconds of sound, biblical reason.

The First Work

The Bible tells us that God created a beautiful garden called Eden and placed Adam there to live (Gen. 1:8-15). But there is nothing to indicate that this garden would remain beautiful on its own. Rather, God put Adam into the garden to cultivate and maintain its splendor. In other words, God gave work for the man to do, and He did so before Adam knew sin. So it is clear that God created the concept of work, and that it was a blessing from the beginning. How wonderful it must have been to till and keep the bounty of Eden! Adam was indeed blessed with such a privilege to work.

Knowing that God created work to be a blessing is good news! There are too many lazy, complaining young men who would like to make you and I think that work is a bad thing, and they will do almost anything to avoid it. And we lament to say that there are also lazy men who are advanced in years, men who have never learned the satisfaction associated with work. Such people are a sorry sight. I like the fact that God made work, for I know that we don't need to feel badly for enjoying it.

What exactly was it like to work in the garden? Well, we will really never know, but I am certain that the work required an effort. But that effort must have been a rewarding one, for it was in this same garden that Adam got to name the animals and eat from the trees to sustain him. Later in the garden, God made the most wonderful of all His creations when He created Eve. I'll bet Adam was proud of the work he had done in the garden when he first showed it to her.

Work and the Curse

Sometime after the creation of Eden, Adam and Eve did the unfathomable; they rebelled against God by eating from the tree of the knowledge of good and evil after God had told them not to. There is much to this rebellion that we do not fully understand, but it is sufficient to know that it was no small mistake. Their act caused a chain reaction of events that affected the world forevermore, and among these effects was the way in which man did work.

The Bible tells us that as a result of Adam and Eve's sin, several things were cursed, and among these was the very ground that Adam had tilled. Along with the good herbs and fruits, thorns and thistles now grew. And God had told Adam that "In the sweat of thy face shall thou eat bread" (Gen. 3:18-19).

It is likely that the thistles and thorns made Adam's work somewhat harder, but to what degree we do not know. We do know that Adam and his offspring would be required to work in order to eat, and this has never since changed.

Work—Still a Blessing

While many things changed as a result of the first sin, some things did not. One thing clearly did not change, and that is that God did not remove the blessing from work for those who would look for it. On the contrary, we know from Scripture that God-given work continued to be a blessing. Solomon knew what hard work was, and he declared, "There is nothing better for a man than to eat and drink and tell himself that his labor is good. This also I have seen, that it is from the hand of God" (Eccl. 2:24). So work is a blessing, and only the lazy fool would think otherwise.

We encourage you to observe the various men whom you admire. Perhaps some of these are your father's friends or your friends' fathers. If you admire them, then it is likely that you can see that they all have at least one thing in common, and that is that they are all hard workers. Who doesn't appreciate a hard worker? Hard work is the backbone of our country and of the good cities and towns that populate it. In fact, hard work is the very backbone of a real man. While a real man must have other qualities, he cannot be said to be virtuous without being dedicated to his work.

Any young man with a sense about him knows that there is a strange yet wonderful pleasure associated with working. It is not the kind of satisfaction one experiences while playing Frisbee or riding a good roller coaster, but is satisfaction nonetheless. In fact, it is a deep satisfaction, the kind that brings well-being, physical health, and restful sleep. And to be sure, there is even associated with hard work the not too rare occasion to have fun. But too many boys confuse satisfaction with having fun. It is the silly boy who thinks he is not taking pleasure unless he is skipping around in playful glee. That is perhaps the way of toddlers and spoiled brats, but it is not the way of well-rounded, young men.

Consider the Sloth

Perhaps the best way to understand the blessing of work is to understand how awful and cursed it is not to work. The Bible has several things to say about this. In some places, it calls the lazy man who does not work a sluggard, which is something akin to a snail without a shell. In other places, the Bible compares a lazy man to a sloth. In case you didn't know, a sloth is an odd looking animal that doesn't do much except eat and sleep while hanging from all four legs in a tree. Scientists who have studied sloths have determined that these creatures will only move if they absolutely have to, and in some cases they may die when food is still within climbing or walking distance. Any way you cut it, neither a sloth nor a sluggard is a good thing to be compared to. Of all the passages on this topic, this one is perhaps the most telling: "The sluggard buries his hand in the dish, and will not even bring it back to his mouth" (Prov. 19:24).

Being a Great Worker

What does it mean to be a great worker? A great worker is not someone who merely exerts a lot of effort, for what good does it do to put forth a strain if you are not diligent and efficient in your efforts? Moreover, what good does it do if a man is diligent and efficient, but is not always dependable? What if he is all of these things but does not have a good attitude? So we can see that being a great worker involves quite a few qualities, and all of these are certainly within your reach. Quite possibly you already have some or all of these qualities. Regardless, let's spend some time studying each of these traits so we can be sure we have a good understanding of its importance:

Exertion

A good worker is someone who is not afraid to strain, and is in fact someone who is glad to do so. If you are working and begin to feel a strain that makes you tired, are you going to quit? For heaven's sake, man, we hope not! Keep on pressing; you will not break. If you are lifting something that is more than you can handle, be sure of your assessment before you set it down. Sometimes you simply need better leverage. Study the body mechanics of the older men, and you may learn a thing or two on how to make your body do what you want.

You should know that your leg muscles are the strongest in your body, but your mind will not always believe it. For this reason, learn to bend at the knees when lifting something that is on the ground, and avoid using your lower back. Put your legs to work, and you may be surprised! When you feel you are at your limit, you still likely have muscle left to spare. As is the case with most of your muscles, you do not yet truly know your limits, for you are growing nearly every day, and your mind does not yet know what you can do.

You should be encouraged to know that the more you work, the stronger you will become, for by work do your muscles grow. Do you see the man with power in his arms, his back, his thighs? He did not get that way by accident. It was with purpose, and to be sure it involved exertion from work.

So press on, young man! Show your stuff! Let the Lord and those for whom you are working know that you want to push yourself to your true limits. Be glad for what you can do, knowing that your efforts are being put into service for others. Take pride in your work, and you will be off to a great start at becoming a great worker.

Diligence

It is one thing to be willing and able to exert yourself, but it is another to continue on with your work until it is completed, or time to quit as determined by whoever is in authority over you. More than one supervisor has been discouraged to see a young man start the day by putting his back into his work, only to have him poop out after a short time. Don't be asking for a drink every so often, and you should only go to the bathroom if you really need to. If you need to take a drink, then be quick about it and get back to work. Don't be afraid to resume work without your supervisor telling you; go right back to your task, and you will make him proud.

We once saw a man who, after every fifteen minutes or so, would take off his tool belt, go to the water cooler, and wash his hands of the dust that he thought was on them. His strange habit caused him to lose momentum which cost his supervisor time and money. This same habit eventually became the cause for his dismissal. In other words, he got fired. He simply wasn't diligent in his work. If you have any kind of habit such as the one this odd fellow had, you would do well to get rid of it at your next opportunity.

When you are working and approaching quitting time, set a reasonable goal for completion, and then meet that goal. Work more rather than less, and you will be the better man for it. Encourage others to do the same, and your enthusiasm will help to carry the moment.

Efficiency

The man who is willing to exert himself and is diligent is on his way to being a great worker, but he is not there yet, for he must also be efficient at what he does. Imagine a man who is hired to dig a hole in some sand. This man works all day non-stop in doing so, but after nine hours has almost nothing to show for it because he didn't know how to throw the sand to the side. Such a man may be commended for his diligence, but he can also be criticized for his lack of knowledge.

You must, to the best of your ability, learn how to be efficient. Learn how to get things done in the quickest manner possible. This may involve learning how to complete more than one task at a time, learning how to run power equipment, or learning how to plan and prepare for the day. The ability to carefully plan is always a great trait. Don't always leave it to the boss to tell you what you will need; think ahead, and you will impress him while making yourself more valuable.

To be sure, there will be times when you are thinking that a way of doing a task is not efficient, but your supervisor may want it done his way anyway. This is not a time to be insistent on your way. If appropriate, you may offer a suggestion in the way of efficiency, but you will do well to gladly comply with whatever response he might give.

"Work smart, not hard" is an oft quoted saying. If you can be efficient while reducing your exertion, then good, but sometimes efficiency requires exertion. Just be willing to exercise all the traits that make a great worker, and soon you will be one if you are not so already.

Dependability

This one probably goes without saying, but we will include it anyway. Simply put, you must be dependable. How disappointing to find an otherwise hard worker who is efficient, but his diligence too often suddenly stops. He may be the world's best worker three days in a row, but he sleeps in on the fourth. Or perhaps he suddenly surprises his supervisor by announcing, "Hey Boss, I have to leave in a half hour. I have an appointment somewhere else." Such a man is an irritant rather than a help. He will never be considered a great worker, and may in fact never even be considered a good worker.

If you are not able to report to work, give your supervisor ample notice, at least two weeks if possible.

If you feel a cold coming on, it is probably better to report to work a little under the weather than to take the whole day off. Sometimes working through a slight cold or other ailment is the best cure for whatever is trying to get at you.

For goodness' sake, don't sleep in! Set your alarm early when you know that work is in store. Getting ready for your day with time to spare is a great way to start.

In short, don't ever give reason to let your supervisor down. Be dependable, and make him proud.

Good Attitude

If you are the type of boy who has a habit of sulking (even if it's just a little) when called into duty, then we can accurately peg you as a boy with a bad attitude. In short, you must see this as wrong, both morally and socially. A bad attitude is considered sinful, and it makes for an uncomfortable environment for everyone around.

Be cheerful when called into duty, and remain so throughout the duration of the job. Just as a bad attitude can be contagious, so can a good attitude. Who doesn't like a person with a good attitude, someone who wants to work and is glad to do so? Among other things, it promotes efficiency and others' ability to be diligent. It can be said that a good attitude makes the whole day go well.

It bears mentioning that a good attitude can actually be carried too far if certain kinds of people are not careful. Such can be the case if a worker is too cheery. Most supervisors can describe workers they have hired who were so cheery that they were always laughing and carrying on, to the point where they couldn't be serious with their work. You will do well to have a cheerful countenance, but do not confuse this with the tendency to be giddy and silly. Keep the topic of conversation limited to the work at hand, unless there are obvious moments where this is not required and your supervisor does not mind. Be serious with your work, act professionally, and you will bring honor to those for whom you are working.

You should not act disrespectfully toward someone you are working for, especially in the presence of others. If you cannot respect the person for whom you are working because he or she is asking you to partake in sinful behavior, then notify your parents. Your mother or father will be able to give you wise counsel in this regard.

It may be possible that sometime through life you will find yourself working in an environment where very few if any of the workers have a good attitude. You may even find that their bad attitudes have a way of rubbing off on you. We of course encourage you to share the love and power of Christ with them, but if you ultimately find yourself being influenced by them negatively, you may simply want to quit this job and find another.

The importance of a good attitude cannot be overemphasized. It is the most important of all work related virtues, for by it the others may come.

Be a Problem Solver

Too many people think they are doing their parents or another authority figure a favor by announcing problems. The boy declares, "Hey, Mom, the toilet is clogged again!" The worker announces, "Hey Boss, we are out of nails and we will need them first thing in the morning." Both the boy and the worker identified a problem, but that is all they did. A great worker does more than this.

A great worker is quick to see problems, but he is even quicker at solving them. Any parent or anyone else in authority will absolutely love a young man for his ability to be a problem solver. The insightful and industrious boy says, "Hey Mom, the toilet was clogged, but I fixed it." The industrious and creative worker says, "Hey Boss, we are almost out of nails, so I will pick some up in the morning and bring them to work." You get the idea. A great worker is a problem solver, not simply a problem announcer.

Working for Hire

Part of becoming a man is learning how to work for pay. You will learn about how to make and spend money wisely in another lesson, but first you need to know a few things about working for money.

First, we advise you to know how much you will be making before you go to work. The exception is if you really do not care because you want to do someone a favor. But if you are working for pay, then it is appropriate that you and your employer agree how much you will be making.

We know of two boys who raked an entire lawn full of leaves for a neighbor lady according to her wishes. The boys had no idea how much they would be paid because the subject never came up. After a job well done, they came to collect. Imagine their surprise and their utter disappointment when the lady gave them only fifty cents each!

How do you make sure that the matter of money is settled? In most instances, whoever is hiring you will let you know how much he is willing to pay, or he will at least bring the subject up. He may in fact ask you how much you want to be paid. Be prepared to give a forthright answer.

You may be in the uncomfortable position of someone hiring you without the subject of compensation coming up. In this case it is best to respectfully bring the subject up. We suggest this approach or one similar to it: "Excuse me, sir (or whatever title is appropriate), would you mind letting me know how much I will be paid? Doing so will help me plan my budget." Most people will be glad to answer such a question. You will need to determine if you are satisfied with the answer.

How should you act when the person for whom you are working pays you? For one, don't count the money in front of him to see if it is all there, and if you are given a check, don't read it to see if it is written for the proper amount. Looking at the money right away can give the impression that you care more about earning than serving, and it may even convey the fact that you do not trust the employer to pay you an appropriate amount. You may assume that the money given you is the correct amount, and you should immediately proceed to thank the employer for the opportunity to work. You can even tell him or her words to the effect that it is a pleasure to serve. We will say that you should notify your employer immediately in the unlikely event he or she shortchanges you. Any good employer would want to know right away so as to make it good with you. Of course, if you are given too much, you should assume it was by mistake. Alert the employer and refund the money.

No One's Business

Once you have agreed on a wage with your employer, then you will do well to not let anyone else on the job know how much you are making. Sharing this information never seems to help anyone involved. The one making less may be tempted to get jealous, while the one making more may be tempted to get haughty.

The wage you agreed to is between you and your employer. If you are not satisfied with it, ask for a raise or try to better your condition with a different job.

A Final Thought

The day will soon come, if it has not already, whereby someone will be working for you. What kind of worker will you want under your watch? Consider this question, and put into action the answers that you would want for yourself. This, of course, is part of the Golden Rule, and you will do well to let it be part of your guide toward being a great worker.

TELEO SCOUTS
Completion In Christ

Made for Service

In a previous lesson, you learned a lot about what it takes to be a great worker. Perhaps you have even had time since then to implement and practice some of the things you have learned. If so, terrific!

The Bible tells us that we should do all things "as unto the Lord," and of course this includes work. This means that you should do your work, no matter what it is, as if you were doing it directly for Jesus Himself. In this regard, Jesus told us that to whatever extent we behave toward others, we do also toward Him (Matt. 25:31-46). So regardless for whom you are working, you should consider yourself working for Christ. This should be enough to admonish you to work hard while also having a great attitude.

While you will be in fact working for the Lord, it is quite practical to realize that you are also working for someone else. At times you may be working for yourself, but more often you will be working for someone or a group of people like a neighbor, a family member, your church, or a boss. If you are self-employed, you will be working for your customers. In each of these instances you should think of yourself as being a servant to the person or people for whom you are working. Consider those for whom you work more highly than you do yourself, and in doing so you will fulfill the Lord's will.

A Servant's Heart

Considering yourself a servant to others will go a long way. For starters, Jesus said it is the way toward greatness (Matt. 20:26-27). This is really quite a different way of thinking than what the world would make you think. Most people who do not know Christ look out for number one, namely themselves, and the idea of serving others may not even enter into their thinking. But this is not the way that it should be with you. You are to serve, and in doing so you will be great in the eyes of the Lord.

What does it mean to have a servant's heart? For sure it includes everything involved with being a great worker, but it also includes more than that. It means that you are truly looking out for others' best interests. It means that you want them to be pleased with your services. It means that you are glad when they are pleased. And it means that you want to please them even more.

The key to having a servant's heart is simply a willingness to serve. One of the best examples in the Bible was when the prophet Isaiah heard the voice of the Lord asking, "Whom shall I send, and who will go for Us?" To this question Isaiah enthusiastically replied, "Here am I, Send me!" (Isa. 6:8). You and I should be ready to respond likewise.

Really, having a servant's heart is not all that hard. Ask anyone who likes to serve what the hardest part is, and he or she will likely tell you that there isn't enough time to get all the serving done! So you will need to know when to serve and when not to serve, but figuring this out will not be too hard if you keep your priorities in order.

Priorities

Priorities are those things in your life that have the most importance. You really cannot be a great server unless you know how to prioritize. Thankfully the Bible gives us clear direction as to how to do so.

Honoring Your Parents

For starters, the Bible indicates that as young men under your parents' authority, you are to serve them first. Too many children think that they are the only ones who are supposed to be served, but the Bible does not support this selfish notion. Your parents have already given you life, fed you, wiped your dirty nose, and changed enough diapers to fill a dump trunk. You should not feel as though they should serve you forever. That being said, they love you enough to meet most of your desires, and the ones they don't meet are not worth the fret for your apparent lack.

Let your heart be filled with the desire to serve your parents, and you will be their greatest delight. It is not likely they will ever take advantage of you in this regard, and to be sure you will be on your way to greatness for your efforts. But don't let greatness be your aim. Greatness is the kind of thing you should accept if it comes, and the truly great don't really even know that they are so.

So do your chores and fulfill your duties, your roles, and your responsibilities. Make your parents' satisfaction your greatest aim, and you will be pleasing them as well as your Heavenly Father.

One day your parents will be older and will perhaps not be able to fully take care of themselves. You will do well to purpose in your heart as a young man to take care of them to the best of your ability in their golden years.

Your Church

Some people fret about who should take priority in regard to needs, the Church or non-believers. Thankfully the Bible gives us an answer. Paul tells us in Galatians, "So then, while we have opportunity, let us do good to all men, and especially to those who are of the household of the faith" (6:10). So God wants us to consider the Church as a priority. This should not come as too big of a surprise, for God want the Church to be healthy so that we can in turn help others.

Your Family

Do not let your family members go without being served in some way often by you. You can pray for them, call on them, encourage them, or assist them with practical needs. We hope in doing so, you will find a fellowship with your siblings that is deep and rewarding.

Keep in mind that the other young men in your Teleo Scout group (if you are fortunate to be in one) are in fact your true brothers in a very real, spiritual sense. So treat them as brothers and serve them accordingly. When they are glad, let yourself be likewise glad so as to share in their joy. When they are sad, let yourself carry their burden so as to lighten their load. Pray for them, encourage them, and above all, be proud of them.

Your Boss

Your boss is the one for whom you will one day be working for pay, if you have not begun doing so already. He or she may also be called your supervisor, crew chief, or manager. The terms really mean pretty much the same thing. This person is the one who gives you instructions and duties to follow, and you are to do things his or her way in whatever manner is prescribed. To be sure, you will have bosses that you absolutely love, and others you only tolerate. But in all regards you can love to serve them. Do so with all the qualities of a good worker, and you will go far.

All Others

In regard to all others, let the Lord place on your heart various desires to serve, and follow those desires. If you want to serve your neighbor, then do so. If you would rather serve a different neighbor, then do so. The good Lord knows you can't be everywhere at the same time, and so don't fret too much about not serving someone if you don't have sufficient time. The important thing is that you remain sensitive to the Holy Spirit's prompting when it comes to the issue of serving others. Listen to His voice, and you will find that your time and efforts will be richly blessed.

When to Not Serve

This lesson may leave you with the idea that you are called to serve no matter what. Indeed, we are called and are privileged to serve more than not, but there are times when we should refrain from serving.

In short, there will be times when you may be dealing with contentious people that want to promote tension rather than peace. While you should at a moment's notice give them grace if they ask for it, you should not feel obliged to serve them. Doing so may only cause them to be enabled, which means you are actually encouraging and empowering them to continue in their selfish ways. Jesus said, "Do not give what is holy to dogs, and do not throw your pearls before swine, lest they trample them under their feet, and turn and tear you to pieces" (Matt. 7:6).

We therefore caution you not to continue serving those who do not appreciate your efforts. You are serving so as to show others Christ, and when it becomes clear that you will not win someone over through servitude, then we encourage you to direct your efforts to others who may be more appreciative. In doing so, you may need to resist the temptation that you are the one at fault. A person with a servant's heart, who loves truth and desires righteousness to prevail, is rarely at fault. There is a lot in this regard that we cannot offer in the way of advice, for each situation will warrant a careful analysis.

Receiving Tips

You should know how to act if someone you are serving offers you a tip. If you are working for hire at a job where tips are common (such as being a waiter or a caddy), then you should graciously accept a tip with proper gratitude. However, if you are working for someone where a tip is not expected, you should decline the tip, regardless of whether or not you are working for hire. Some would instruct that this should be the end of the matter, and that you should never accept a tip for a good deed under any circumstance. We do not counsel this, for we know that there may be times when refusing a tip can actually be offensive to somebody.

When you decline a tip, do so graciously. You may want to say something like, "Oh, no, you don't need to offer me anything; I am glad to do the work. Thank you, but allow me to decline."

The person offering you the tip will do one of two things. He will either put his money away and graciously accept your offer to decline, or he will let you know that he really wants you to accept the tip. He may respond by asking, "Are you sure? I would love for you to take this." At this point you may decline again, but if at any point he insists, then you should receive the offer with humble gratitude. Let him know that you are honored.

Keeping Your Word

Our discussion on this matter would not be complete without talking about the importance of keeping your word. If you indicate to someone that you are going to do something, especially in the way of serving, then you can bet that he is planning on you doing so. Your word is the same as a promise. Letting him down by not carrying through with your promise would be wrong. You must do everything in your power to honor and keep your word.

It is best not to give your word in the first place if you suspect that you will not be able to keep it. If you absolutely cannot keep your word after giving it, then you would do well to let the other person know that you regret the situation and that you are sorry for causing an inconvenience. If not keeping your word will cause an inconvenience, you may want to consider offering some alternatives which will help the matter out. Again, try to be a problem solver rather than a problem maker.

Summing It Up

Jesus was the prime example of a quality leader, and He led by serving. In serving, He empowered His disciples by teaching them how to do likewise. He taught through example how to work, how to minister, and how to serve. In short, He taught them how to love, which of course is part of the Golden Rule.

We encourage you to do likewise. We will join you along the way, and may the world be a better place for our efforts.

A Worldview Analysis

Imagine a sailor in the middle of the sea who has only a vague idea of where he came from or where he is going. Moreover, he lacks a sound understanding of the winds, currents, tides, and their cumulative effects upon him. And to top it off, this particular sailor prefers to sail in circles because he thinks that the earth is flat, and so he is forever concerned with going over the edge. Despite his condition, he considers himself a capable seaman, for he is naively unaware of his ignorance. Would you entrust this sailor with the duty of providing safe passage for himself or others? Not likely. Yet such a man represents the state a person is in without a proper understanding and adherence to a correct *worldview*. Though he thinks he is sailing, he is really only drifting.

Right off the bat, you might be wondering what we are talking about when we say "worldview." Don't worry—many adults don't even know what this expression is, for they simply haven't given it much thought. However, an understanding of worldview is vital to being a mature man.

There are all kinds of worldviews, and we are going to discuss some of them in our lesson. But before we do that, let's take the time to define our subject matter:

What's the "World"?

As you suspect, "worldview" has something to do with viewing the world. But what do we mean when we refer to the "world"? It might surprise you that we are not merely talking about the planet Earth. Nor are we broadening our meaning by only including the various continents and oceans that comprise the earth, although these may come into play. Rather, we are referring to God's creation in its entirety, which of course includes the human race created in His image. So when referring to the "world," we place a special emphasis on mankind.

When we consider mankind as part of the world, we are very much interested in how he thinks. How he thinks determines a lot of things, not the least of which is his view of God. In this regard, we are not talking about anything that is *tangible*, that is, anything you can see, hear, touch, or otherwise sense. For this reason, you might have to tighten your thinking cap, but we will try to make this as easy to understand as we can.

"World" + "View"

As you know, the common definition of "view" refers to the perspective or vantage point from which a person sees things. For example, your dog would look like a huge, hairy monster if you viewed him from only one inch away, but he would hardly be detectable if you viewed him from a mile away. The sun looks smaller than the moon when viewed from the earth, but we all know the sun is many times larger than the moon.

Because people see things from many different vantage points, there can be apparent contradictions in what people see, when in fact there aren't contradictions at all. For example, one person might describe a coin as being relatively smooth with having only the image of a bison. Another person, having never seen this side of the coin, thinks this description is crazy, for he sees only the image of an Indian chief. Still a third person sees no image at all, viewing only the edge and its many ridges. Only when each person sees all sides of the coin can an agreement be made on what the coin really looks like. But even then there will be subtle differences of opinion.

And remember the aimless sailor of our introduction? He thinks the earth is flat because it appears so upon initial observation, but he shouldn't need to be shown a photo taken from outer space to see that he is wrong. If he were to only study the horizon, he would see a ready curve, and he might also see the tips of ship masts coming toward him before he saw their hulls. With proper facts and a little reasoning, he should be able to conclude that the earth is indeed a sphere.

Our definition of "view" changes somewhat when we use the term "view" in relation to worldview. In this usage, view refers to the perspective or vantage point from which a person considers or *thinks about* things. This is especially true in regard to *abstract* things, which are things that can't be seen with your eyes or heard with your ears—things like freedom, love, growing up, fatherhood, and God, just to name a few. For example, you have viewed the concept of growing up from the vantage point of being in your family, and you have viewed the concept of death based on your observations and knowledge about this subject.

By now you may have figured it out: Your views about all the various things in the world, all added up together, make up your *worldview*. Another definition of worldview might be "the final conclusion of all your thoughts about the world."

No Two Worldviews Alike

It is safe to say that there are no two worldviews exactly alike. The more experiences two or more people share, the greater the likelihood they will have similar worldviews. But even then, there is no guarantee in this regard. Take for example a set of twins raised together in the same household. When each of the twins grows up, one might think that politics is the most important thing in the world, but the other may think that voting is a waste of time.

How can it be that there are no two worldviews exactly alike? The answer is really simple. For one, there is no way that two or more people can be raised exactly alike. In the case of our twins, one twin may have shaken the hand of the President himself and been forever inspired. The other may have been forced to watch boring reruns of the Whitewater scandal and been forever put off. So we can see that our experiences significantly influence our worldview.

But just as important, we must be aware that God made us to be creatures of choice. In other words, we have a free will, and the thousands upon thousands of choices that we make in response to our experiences add up and therefore influence our worldview. For example, one brother might choose to be jealous of a friend who got a new bike for Christmas, while the other brother might choose to be glad for the friend. These single choices may then significantly affect the eventual worldview that each brother will develop.

How Cultures Form

Even though there are no two worldviews exactly alike, there are plenty of times when a large number of people think enough alike that the people can be identified accordingly. A large group of people with similar worldviews in this regard are said to be of the same *culture*. For example, American culture is perceived worldwide as a collection of people who generally have ample money generated from jobs which are part of a competitive economy. The people of this culture are considered ambitious and lovers of both work and entertainment. Russian culture, on the other hand, is often perceived as a collection of people who generally are not wealthy and who may in fact be struggling financially as a result of government mandates to collect and redistribute wealth. The people of this culture are not considered overly joyful and are often known for their rather melancholy dispositions. In these examples, are the characteristics of each culture applicable to all the people within each culture? Certainly not, and in fact the most we can really say is that these characteristics are *stereotypes*, or impressions which may or may not be true. In fact, there are some terribly poor segments within American culture, and there are many well-to-do Russians who are genuinely joyous for all kinds of good reasons.

Subcultures

It is important to note that there are often many *subcultures* within a culture. For example, in America there is what we call a Baby-Boomer generation, which is a culture of people born in the mid-1940's to the early 60's who are characterized as an individualistic generation with a tendency to reject authority. Relatively well educated, they are generally spenders rather than savers, who liberally use credit to finance purchases. This might oversimplify them, but you get the picture. And within this single subculture there are other subcultures. For example, much of the vegetarian subculture is part of the Baby Boomer culture, and this subculture has its own peculiarities and stereotypes.

We could cite countless examples of various cultures and subcultures, and in fact entire professions are devoted to studying them. What is important to you, however, is that you understand that cultures and subcultures arise in part from the evolving worldviews that take shape when similar people think similarly.

The Importance of the Matter

Everyone has a worldview whether he realizes it or not. It simply can't be helped; if a person has conclusions based upon the sum of his thinking, then he has a worldview. So then, if there are as many worldviews as there are people, then it is safe to say that not all of these can be correct. Indeed, the Bible makes this clear: "There is a way which seems right to a man, but its end is the way of death" (Prov. 14:12).

The reasons are many as to why false views exist. But common to them all is the fact that most people see the world through faulty lenses. Their lenses cause distortions in everything they see, and so therefore they are unable to make proper conclusions. They are like the astronomer, who, upon looking through his telescope, concludes that the moon and all the planets in our solar system are covered with huge cracks, when in truth he is looking through shattered lenses. Ignorant that his telescope was dropped at the factory, he reports his findings to fellow colleagues who applaud his conclusions and pass his findings on as facts.

Consider the myriad ways that false worldviews can mess up a person's ability to see reality. A young lady wants to dedicate her life to saving all animals because she has concluded they are equal to humans. A young man thinks all rich people are evil because he let jealousy or resentment set in as a boy. There is another young lady who never wants to get married because all she saw growing up were parents that were fighting. Elsewhere, a young man grows up wanting to murder others not of his religion because that is what he thinks God requires of him.

Left unchecked, false worldviews have a way of multiplying. It's as the old adage says, "Birds of a feather flock together." The girl who wants to save the lives of all animals has only to find a sympathetic ear, and soon she has another voice to promote her cause. The young man who thinks all rich people are evil may form a hate-the-upper-class club. It doesn't take long before incorrect thinking adds up and forms a cultural worldview, resulting in a very confused and troubled society.

The people we have described are, in a very real sense, "blind" to reality. God sent His Son, Jesus, as a remedy for this predicament. Jesus said, "For judgment I came into this world, so that those who do not see may see…" (John 9:39). It is clear throughout Scripture that we are called to carry on the work of Christ. Jesus said, "Let your light shine before men…" (Matt. 5:16). Why would He have us do this if it were not to help others see? In His Great Commission, Jesus told his disciples, "Go and make disciples of all the nations…. teaching them to observe all that I commanded you" (Matt. 28:20), so it is clear that it is up to us to help present reality to the world. And God will open up the eyes of those who want to see so that they will in turn share the good news of reality with others.

Truth & Reality—The Christian Worldview

There is much that can be said in regard to perspective, but none more important than the fact that God has the most accurate perspective on all matters. After all, it is He who is *omniscient*, meaning that He knows all things that can be known. If He knows the words that are forming on your lips before you utter them (Psalm 139:4), as well as the number of hairs on your head (Matt. 10:30), then you can rest assured that His perspective is an accurate one. In fact, if you are ever attempting to understand the reality of any subject, you would do well to consider what God's perspective is on the matter.

The following is a summary of what all true Christians believe. If you equate yourself with Jesus Christ, then these are the tenets of your faith and the foundation of your worldview. You would do well to understand your worldview deeply and fully, for it is far more important than knowing your ABC's or being able to tie your shoes:

Divine Revelation

At the core of our worldview, we as Christians believe that

God discloses His perspective through *divine revelation*. In other words, He supernaturally lets mankind know what He is thinking. In the days of old, He did this primarily by way of the Torah, which are the first five books of the Old Testament and the foundation for the Law of Moses. After the Torah became established and taught, God continued to reveal His will through the judges and the prophets, and their writings in part comprise the rest of the Old Testament.

Throughout the Old Testament, we see a common thread in God letting His people know that one day a Savior would be provided to them. This Savior would fulfill the Law and rule His people for all of eternity. Justice, grace, and mercy would be afforded through Him to all the nations of the earth, and He would be called "God is With Us" by those who followed his rule (Isa. 7:14, Matt. 1:23). Christians believe that God's promise was fulfilled through the birth of Jesus Christ into the world.

Through Jesus Christ, God completed His divine revelation to us. Jesus Himself said, "He who has seen Me has seen the Father" (John 14:9), and the Apostle Paul elaborated by writing, "For in [Jesus] all the fullness of Deity dwells in bodily form" (Col. 2:9). Jesus indicated pointedly that His teaching was God's revelation, "... the word which you hear is not Mine, but the Father's who sent Me" (John 14:24). The Bible describes Jesus as being the "Word," signifying that all meaning is derived from Him (John 1:1). So Christians believe that if we want to know what God's revelation is, we only need to study the life of Jesus Christ.

As Christians, we also believe that the teachings of Jesus Christ and His first disciples are recorded accurately in the New Testament, beginning with the gospels, which are the four biographies of Jesus, and ending with the book of Revelation. The New Testament, together with Old Testament, comprise the Bible, which Christians believe is the written Word of God.

There are other religions that claim to have direct revelation from God, but none that make the same claims that Jesus does. Among other things, Jesus stated, "I am the way, and the truth, and the life; no one comes to the Father but through Me" (John 14:6). So as C.S. Lewis succinctly deduced, we are pressed to choose between believing Him or thinking Him to be a madman or a liar. Jesus gave us good reason to believe Him, not the least of which was His sacrificial death on a cross followed by His glorious resurrection. We encourage you to study further regarding the certainty and validity of Jesus' claims, for doing so will only solidify your existing faith.

Mankind, Purposefully Created

As part of our worldview, we also believe that God created the world purposefully, and that He did so out of nothing. And in doing so, He ultimately created men and women in His image. Christians reject the idea that mankind somehow evolved accidentally by random chance or luck. Christians assert that without intelligent design, even simple life could not have formed, let alone human beings with all their complexity.

We also believe that God is intimately involved with His creation. He did not merely create mankind and then leave him completely to his own devices. Rather, God cares for mankind and desires fellowship with him.

Sin, a Separator

Christians believe that God is holy, meaning that He is pure, righteous, and perfect. And because God made man in His image, man was created also being pure, righteous, and perfect. However, as Genesis states, mankind disobeyed God, causing separation from his Maker. You see, only a person who is holy can commune with Holiness, and disobedience is everything holiness is not. God expected mankind to abide by the standard that He set forth, yet man chose to not obey.

Throughout Scripture, disobedience and all similar attitudes and behaviors, like rebellion and selfishness, are called *sin*. According to the Bible, sin has infected the world, so much so that each man and woman alive has sinned at some point in his or her life (Rom. 5:12). According to the Bible, the result of sin is death (Rom. 6:3).

Jesus Christ, the Remedy for Sin

In our previous lesson called "Loving Righteousness and Hating Sin," we discussed the part of the Christian worldview which believes that ever since man's first rebellion, there has been the historical need to be reconciled with God as a result of sin. If you missed that lesson, you would do well to study it at your next opportunity.

In short, the Christian worldview recognizes that Jesus Christ fulfilled the whole Law of the Old Testament, so much so that He took the sins of mankind upon Himself. The Bible reveals that Jesus sacrificed His body upon a cross, and that His death was completed when He actually became sin (Rom. 8:3-4). As a result of this sacrifice, He provided the one and only way to God.

Christians believe also that Jesus Christ did not remain dead; rather, He rose from the grave after three days (1 Cor. 15:4), and that He is seated at the right hand of His Father in Heaven while ruling those who believe on His name (Luke 22:69). After His resurrection, Jesus sent His Holy Spirit to guide, direct, convict, and impart power to those who would believe on His name (John 16:7-13).

Lastly, our worldview embraces the belief that Jesus Christ will return again to bring final judgment upon the world. In this regard, Christians assert that those who have placed faith in Jesus will live and reign eternally with Him, but not so for those who have rejected His sacrifice (John 3:18).

Some Common, False Worldviews

If we are to be mature, well-rounded men, it is useful to be aware of some of the worldviews which have influenced our culture. The following are some of the more common ones; a book would be required to cover them all in depth. For the purposes of our study, we have categorized these worldviews as being either religious or non-religious:

Religious Worldviews

Religious worldviews have a couple of things in common. For starters, they hold that there are one or more universal gods, spirits, or divine entities. They also believe that their gods have established an eternal, moral code that can be known (at least in part) by human beings. These worldviews believe that people have a duty to follow the moral codes that their respective gods have revealed. Lastly, they hold that human behavior has long term, after-death significance. As you might realize, Christianity is a religious worldview. But there are several others that are false to the core:

The Muslim Worldview

A Muslim is someone who subscribes to the religion of Islam. Islam believes in one god whose name is Allah. While Muslims claim to believe that the Bible is a holy text, they are either fibbing or do not know what they are talking about, for they do not believe Jesus Christ is the Son of God.

This whole religion came from the musings of a so-called prophet named Muhammad during the early to mid-seventh century. Muhammad liked to hang out in caves for rather long periods of time while giving thought to his religion. He claimed that the angel Gabriel and Allah himself gave him a new revelation to write down and teach to others. These teachings were recorded in the Koran (or Qur'an), which Muslims view as being more holy and important than the Bible.

It might strike you as odd that Muhammad claimed he was visited by the angel Gabriel. We think it odd too, but whether he made this up for effect or was actually visited by some kind of strange spirit we may never know. Regardless, we do know that the message he claimed to have received was *not* from God. The apostle Paul wrote, "But even if we, or an angel from heaven, should preach to you a gospel contrary to what we have preached to you, let him be accursed" (Gal. 1:8). It appears that Muhammad either forgot this important passage or was interested in advancing his own agenda.

There is a long list of sins described within Islam, but there is no provision for remedy in this regard. Rather, a Muslim's hope for Paradise rests in his or her ability to live according to the will of Allah. Central to the will of Allah are daily prayers and rituals as well as one's submission to Islam and willingness to promote it.

Jihad is the term used to describe one's willingness to promote Islam. A fully submitted Muslim is to be willing to exert his utmost power and ability in contending with the "infidel," which is any one or group of people who reject Islam. Many (but not all) Muslims believe that the only way to contend with the so-called infidel is by way of physical force. The terrorist movement against Christians and some entire countries is fueled largely by Muslims who take their sense of Jihad very seriously. They believe Allah wants to eliminate the infidel by whatever means necessary, including death, so as to spread the cause of Islam.

Islam is now arguably the world's largest religion. Much of Africa, the Mid-East, and parts of Asia adhere to its tenets.

The Hindu Worldview

The Hindu religion is one of many forms of Eastern mysticism, so it is mostly prevalent in India and eastern Asia. This worldview believes that there is one divine power, but that this power takes on innumerable forms.

Hindus believe in a sort of spiritual Ferris wheel that never stops. They believe that life and death are cyclical, and that there are three forces (i.e. gods) at work within this cycle: In essence, *Brahma* arises as the start of creation, then *Vishnu* sustains it during growth and inevitable decline, and *Shiva* destroys life so that Brahma can start it all over again. This cycle occurs in all individual life, as well as collective systems, including the entire universe.

Hindus believe that all life is sacred to varying degrees. Their adherence to Shiva allows for some animals to be used as legitimate food sources, but they do consider some animals like cows and bulls so sacred that they are prohibited from consumption. While you and I see T-bones and ribeye steaks on a standing Angus, a Hindu sees an object of prayer and worship.

Hindus believe in *karma*, which is the consequence of one's actions in this present life. Depending on how a person lives, he or she will be reborn after death in either a higher or lower physical form. If one lives properly and attains good karma, he can eventually be reincarnated in a favorable way and perhaps be reunited with the one, divine power.

There is no single sacred text that Hindus adhere to. In fact, there are thousands of variations of Hindu beliefs due to the thousands of gurus (enlightened teachers) who offer unique paths of prayer, study, and meditation.

The Worldview of Buddhism

Buddhism is another form of Eastern mysticism. It is the

result of the teachings of a monk named Buddha in the fifth century B.C. Like Hinduism, Buddhism believes that life and death are cyclical. But it places a special emphasis on the concept of suffering during this cycle.

According to Buddhists, all life results in suffering to varying degrees. Suffering, they argue, is always the result of some kind of craving, so suffering can be avoided by suppressing one's cravings. Suppression in this regard can be attained through a religious, eightfold process. It is only through this process that true happiness can result.

Buddhists also believe that a person can end the cycle of reincarnation by reaching *nirvana.* Nirvana is a state of total freedom, where one no longer must be reborn, and can be attained through a proper accumulation of *dharma* (true knowledge) and appropriate, moral living.

If Hinduism and Buddhism seem a bit mystical and even spooky, it is because they are. There is an uncertainty in much of what these religions attempt to attain. Depending on how the gods reward your karma, you may in one life be a king, but in another life you may be a housefly. Look out—that may be your great granddad who is dodging your flyswatter!

New Age Worldview (Spiritualism)

The various forms of New Age thinking also have their origins in Eastern mysticism, but they are heavily influenced by a large amount of Western thought.

New Agers believe in a never-ending cycle of life, but they also adhere to *pantheism.* Pantheism is the belief that God is in all, and all is in God. So God can be found in the smallest pebble, the largest tree, an invisible molecule of oxygen, a far away star, and everything in between. Of course, this includes humans and all other forms of life.

There are nearly as many forms of New Age beliefs as there are adherents. Believers of this religion range from those who think the alignment of the stars determines one's future to those who try to get healed using crystals.

It is interesting to note that those involved with New Age practices do not label themselves so. You will probably never hear someone introduce herself by saying, "Hi, I'm Kathy, and I am a New Ager." Rather, the term is usually used by those outside of the movement.

"New Age" is used because those in the movement believe there will one day be a "new age" where there will be a new world order of peace. How do they know this? By the zany belief that the constellation of Aquarius declares it so.

Occultism

Occultism is the study or practice of supernatural or paranormal phenomenon which are not achieved by or through God. This includes but is not limited to astrology, extra sensory perception, magic (other than sleight of hand tricks/illusions), communicating with or praying to the dead, witchcraft, or Satanism.

As you might suspect, the New Age movement involves some occult practices. However, not everyone who practices occultism believes in the Eastern mysticism elements of spiritualism.

Those who practice occultism have the worldview that supernatural and paranormal forces exist and that some kind of personal satisfaction or benefit can be attained through their study or practice. Usually adherents of occultism do not have a lofty social goal such as world peace in mind. Nor are they primarily interested in eternal matters. Rather, they aim for egocentric, temporal experiences which give them a sense of power or amusement.

We have seen too many Christians get spooked over those practicing the occult. It is enough to say that we are not to engage in occult practices, but neither should we fear them. In reality, they are silly and foolish practices, and any so-called spirits associated with them tremble at the mere sound of Jesus' holy name. Rest assured, there is nothing that can take you from the hand of God, and the power of the Holy Spirit within you is more than sufficient to enable you to minister to those caught up in this false worldview (1 John 4:4).

Non-Religious Worldviews

Some people embrace worldviews that claim to deny the existence of God or the ability for God to be known. We will categorize these as being non-religious. It should be pointed out that the distinction between religious and non-religious worldviews is not always clear, for many of the so-called non-religious worldviews are in fact very religious:

Naturalism

Although naturalism has been around in varying forms for hundreds of years, it began to gain momentum during the Enlightenment Period of the seventeenth-century. It is still very much alive today.

A naturalist, for the purposes of our discussion, is someone who does more than study nature. He is someone who believes that nature provided its own origin, that creation and all that is in it came from previous nature, which at one point came from one chunk of non-living mass. How naturalists know this is of course a matter of faith, but they don't seem to think this is a religion.

Those who adhere to naturalism do not believe in God. In this regard, they are *atheists*. They have no convictions in regard to God or eternal matters, believing simply that nature is all there is to this world. The atheistic mindset is a sorry one indeed. It reminds us of the proverb, "The fool has said in his heart, 'There is no God.'" (Prov. 1:14).

Naturalists deny the existence of spirit, divine or otherwise. In their thinking, matter is all that exists, and the universe is a closed, fixed system which functions only by cause and effect. And because matter is all that exists, human thought and sensations are simply the mechanistic result of atoms in the brain. Man is therefore nothing more than a machine or a highly developed animal. Some even go so far as to believe that all of human behavior is governed by natural forces, and that humans have no free will. This belief, unique in its own right, is called *behaviorism*.

As you might guess, this line of thinking considers death to be a final state. A dead man is nothing more than a memory in the mind of the living. He is no longer good for anything other than worm food. Neither his personality nor his spirit lives on. If this sounds kind of depressing, that's because it is.

Naturalists believe that all moral laws, values, and ethics originate and exist in the mind of man. There is no universal moral law giver (i.e. God), so accordingly there cannot be any moral absolutes. This line of thinking has ushered in the concept of *moral relativism* which prevails in our culture today. Moral relativism states that morals and values are only useful and valid to the degree that they benefit certain individuals and societies.

Humanism

During the Enlightenment, people began to adhere to the belief that truth could be attained by way of human reason. This belief emerged primarily due to the relatively large progress that science was enjoying as a new discipline of study. You see, prior to this time, science as an empirical, systematic means of study was not largely practiced. With the advent of inventions like the telescope and the new mathematics postulated by Copernicus and Newton, all kinds of theories and discoveries were being made.

Some scientists, like Newton, advanced the new sciences as a means of understanding the creative genius of God. Unfortunately, however, many people began to elevate human reason above all else. Their use of the new sciences and their resulting discoveries birthed a new form of arrogance. The "enlightened" culture held to the notion that science was the key to all knowledge, and hence, all truth. Moreover, they embraced an unprecedented view of history as one of human progression in a favorable direction. Their faith in science as a means of human progress is one of the key tenets of *humanism*. Although humanism had its roots over three hundred years ago, it is alive and well today.

Humanism, like naturalism, is an atheistic worldview which believes that matter is all that exists. But unlike naturalism, humanism views humanity as being the crowning achievement of the universe's evolution. Humanism believes that humanity will continue to progress and evolve to the point where world peace is a consistent norm. Indeed, a quick study of humanistic literature will indicate that everything from world peace to the eradication of human disease will be the result of human evolution.

We will not refrain in poking a bit of fun at humanism, for we are bewildered as to how they can honestly think that human evolution will bring peace. With the emphasis that they place on the value of empirical study and observation, one would think that they could readily see that the world is at war with itself as much as or more than ever before. So we ask: On what *scientific* basis can they claim that humanity is progressing forward? How can observations in this regard be verifiably measured? The answer on both accounts: it's not possible. Indeed, the idea that the world has gotten more peaceful since the Enlightenment is laughable. While we poke fun at the fact that they claim something so scientifically false, we also hope each person blinded by this worldview will one day clearly see the hypocrisy of his beliefs.

While humanism's great expectation is world peace, it makes no claim for peace beyond death. It cannot, for like naturalism, it denies the existence of the human spirit. Bertrand Russell, one of humanism's best known proponents, was quoted as stating, "There is darkness without and when I die there will be darkness within. There is no splendor, no vastness, anywhere; only triviality for a moment, and then nothing." So like naturalism, humanism's conclusion in regard to death is a depressing one.

We hesitate to categorize humanism as a non-religious worldview. We have done so only because humanism claims there is no God. But in reality their worldview has ironically become their god. After all, they accept many of the tenets of their worldview with a greater measure of unscientific faith than some religions, and thus their worldview can be considered a religious one.

Agnosticism

The word *gnosis* is Greek for "knowledge," so an agnostic is simply someone who believes that God cannot be figured out or known. Some agnostics won't go so far as to state conclusively that God cannot be known, but they will admit their uncertainty on the matter.

On one hand, an agnostic's worldview is somewhat predictable. You can expect that such a person would not believe in an absolute, moral law, so he would probably embrace moral relativism. Also, such a person would generally be tolerant of your beliefs, especially if he is uncertain of his own position.

On the other hand, an agnostic's worldview may not be

predictable, because there really are no common tenets within this worldview. So you can expect agnostics to be as different from one another as any other people group.

Sorting It All Out

If you are normal, you may feel a bit overwhelmed at so many false worldviews. You might be even more overwhelmed by knowing that we did not list them all. If so, it might help to realize that it is not essential that you keep track of them all. And you certainly don't need to feel as though you must properly label or categorize each one you encounter. Doing so would be nearly impossible, for often worldviews overlap. I like how one young man summarized the various, false worldviews. He stated, succinctly, "They're all messed up." That is really all you need to know.

Of course, you should know what you believe and why you believe it. In this regard, we encourage you in your studies. Your study of Jesus Christ and the Christian worldview will only lead you to a closer walk with Him. And while you don't have to obsess with memorizing all the other various philosophies, you will do well to always realize a couple of things from this lesson. First, everyone has a worldview, and knowing about various worldviews will help you to be prepared when you encounter them. Second, your knowledge will help you to understand the vantage point from which other people come. This realization, coupled with love you should have for all men, will help you to always give an answer for the hope that is within you (1 Pet. 3:15)!

A Lesson on Peace

In a previous lesson, we discussed various worldviews and how one's philosophy is shaped by his worldview. In this lesson, we will see that one's concept of peace is no exception to this rule. Indeed, there are several worldviews in regard to peace, but only one is the way to true, everlasting peace, and that is the peace that Jesus offers.

Jesus told His disciples, "Peace I leave with you; My peace I give to you; *not as the world gives, do I give to you*" (John 14:27, emphasis added). So He made it clear that there is more than one kind of peace, and that the peace offered by the world has nothing to do with Him. What is the difference between the kind of peace that Jesus offers and the kind the world offers? Perhaps this can best be answered by first considering some of the erroneous worldviews regarding peace.

Peace—My Way, or Else

Most people agree that peace involves an absence of conflict. But there are differing ideas, mostly wrong ones, as to how peace should be attained. Heading this list is the age-old, selfish idea that if enough force is demonstrated, then others can be subdued to the point where there is no conflict. This approach can be exercised by a single person, as in the case of a playground bully. Or it can be employed by an entire government, like when a tyrannical regime rises to power.

Consider the insecure playground bully who proclaims himself leader of the other boys around him. He may allow others to play games, but only if they play the ones he agrees to. And if he is losing, he will likely change the rules so as to skew the score in his favor. Others may oppose him, but they will not succeed unless they can demonstrate more muscle than he has. Often such a bully will prevail, and as time goes by the others may comply with his rule to the point where they think everything about their situation is normal. In doing so, there may appear to be an absence of conflict. The others may not resist the bully at all, and in fact may even consider him a friend. Regardless, he is no friend, for he has selfishly manipulated them into compliance. The others will hardly be able to think for themselves, and many will in turn bully others when given the opportunity.

In the case above, it may be possible that the other boys' parents are unaware that the bully has made his stand. The playground supervisor may not even be aware, though she daily passes by, for there may appear in this scenario a peaceful setting, boys frolicking in their various games, football one day, Frisbee the next. Unbeknownst, the bully has the others securely under his thumb; they are puppets on his string, robots under his control. But there is no real peace here. Rather, the tension normally evident has been suppressed, like so many penned up dogs who no longer bark under protest, resigning themselves to a life of confinement under their master's rule.

Consider also the governmental ruler who has risen to great power by way of force. He has manipulated more than a playground of boys; he has subdued an entire people group, a nation of constituents which has no choice but to recognize him as its leader. He may be called Governor, King, or Chancellor, but his truthful title is Oppressor. Though there may be a calm during his rule, it is in spite of and not because of it. For while there appears an absence of tension, the spirit of each man yearns for the better form of rule, the way of peaceful, willful submission under a free reign. Did one man come to such power by his own accord? No, not likely, for submission of this kind requires force-times-force. But the Oppressor is able to recruit this force, and is able also to employ it. Indeed, kingdoms of this sort are full the world over, and as each has risen, each will surely fall.

The way toward peace by rule is not the way of the Lord. We caution you to be forever on guard against it.

Peace via Humanism

Recall that you learned a bit about humanism in your last lesson. Humanism, as you learned, is the theory and practice that emphasizes reason, scientific inquiry, and human fulfillment at the expense of rejecting God.

As you also learned, humanists believe in unguided biological evolution. But you should also know they believe in societal evolution. In other words, they believe that humanity is slowly but surely maturing toward a *utopia*, which is a theoretical, perfect place or state on earth where everyone lives in harmony. Humanists believe that mankind should make efforts to promote peace, but they believe these efforts are themselves governed by natural, evolutionary forces.

The humanistic worldview regarding peace is ungodly, and it is laden with ridiculous, optimistic notions. In fact, it is downright silly. Never in the history of man has world peace been the norm, not even during the mythical times of Atlantis or King Arthur. And the world is not getting any more peaceful. In fact, Jesus told us that until He returns there will always be "wars and rumors of wars (Matt. 24:6).

It is not surprising that the humanistic worldview is simply another worldview which conveniently ignores the fact that sin has entered into the human race. In fact, humanists not only ignore the sin issue, they downright reject it. After all, how can sin exist if there is no God?

But the Bible tells us plainly that "…all have sinned and fall short of the glory of God (Rom. 3:23).

Peace via False Religions

There has never been a shortage of false religions in the world. This should be no surprise, for Jesus warned, "…false Christs and false prophets will arise…" (Matt. 24:24). Some of these false worldviews place an emphasis on the concept of peace. Some religions, like Islam, claim to promote peace, but they are among the most violent in both theory and practice. Others, like the cow worshipping Hindu religion, are heavy into mysticism, and they strive to attain peace through ungodly forms of meditation. The Bahai faith foolishly thinks that peace will inevitably come under a one world government that believes as they do.

There are also bizarre and outlandish cults that believe they have the way to peace. Among these are believers of UFO's driven by aliens from outer space that will one day bring world peace to the earth. Some cults, like scientology, believe that man is immortal with unlimited capabilities, and that individual peace can be found through adherence to certain tenets.

Every one of the false religions has failed miserably to bring even a single person true, everlasting peace. We can state this with conviction, for no worldly religion can properly address the tension between God and man caused by sin.

Peace, Hippie Style

During the 1950's an already existing wave of rebellion

among teenagers began to gain momentum, and it has continued to this present day. During the 1960's, this rebellion was defined and manifested in the expression of the teenagers of that time, whom the media and others called "hippies."

Among other things, the hippies were characterized by hanging out with each other in large numbers and wearing bizarre clothing that didn't match. Also, they frequently took illegal drugs to alter their states of mind. "All You Need is Love," "Give Peace a Chance," "If it feels good, do it," and "down with the establishment" were popular song titles and sayings of the times. While they claimed to be supporters of peace, they were in fact blatant hypocrites (a hypocrite is someone who says one thing but in fact believes the opposite as evident by his behavior). Indeed, the hippies were not really peaceful at all, for they despised and strongly resisted nearly all forms of authority, including politicians, policemen, and even their parents. It is a good thing for their sakes they weren't living in the days of Moses under the Law, for they would not have done very well with Deuteronomy 21:18-21!

The hippies really were shallow thinkers. They seemed to reject the idea that evil even existed, and their naïve answer to avoiding all war was to simply stop fighting. They spoke out against governments that supported freedom of choice, but they supported socialistic and communistic governments that oppressed people. The hippies were truly confused, but then again that's what a mix of rebellion and drugs will do to you.

Although we don't use the term "hippie" today, their selfish and ungodly philosophy is still very much alive. You will see it evident in anyone who doesn't believe that evil exists outside of his own country. You will see it expressed in anyone who wants to legalize mind altering drugs, or in anyone who disrespects God's institution of marriage. Often, you will see clues of hippie mentality in those who think that animals are equal to men. Their warped sense of peace has thus caused some to conclude that hunting and fishing are violent and cruel. And don't forget, these people think that peace is the absence of any kind of fighting, so they will not even fight for what is right. Most of the time they will not even acknowledge that there is a right and wrong.

This kind of peace is not God's kind of peace. You will do well to recognize it for what it is, simply a selfish by-product of a false worldview.

Peace by Denial

Shortly after World War II, the worldview of *postmodernism* was quietly ushered in, later to be accelerated by the hippie subculture. Among other things, postmodernism rejects most absolutes and extremes. It basically says that no single voice is the correct one (except, hypocritically, its own). But during the hippie era, postmodernism was not fully mature, which is why the hippies were so vocal in declaring that their philosophy was the correct one. As we stated earlier, their erroneous philosophy is still prevalent today.

It is important to point out that the hippie subculture helped to pave the way for postmodernism's maturity because it clouded our country's then existing ideas of morality. In the decades preceding the hippie era, American culture embraced a fairly strong sense of right and wrong (although we will note that its sense of right and wrong was not always a biblical one). The voice of the hippie subculture shook up the way people thought. Of course, the hippie generation had children of their own who were heavily influenced by their parents' confused philosophy. Ironically, many of the hippies grew up, and upon reflection, admitted that they were overly zealous in their thinking. They began to think that maybe they didn't have all the answers, after all. Meanwhile, some of the older generation began to doubt their own values and convictions. All of this eventually led to the cultural state we are now in, whereby most people are so utterly confused that they deny there even is a problem.

Moral Relativism

Moral relativism is the logical conclusion of postmodernism, but it is selfish and lazy to the core. It is selfish because it is a worldview which conveniences the individual at the expense of others. And it is lazy because it neither takes time to seek God's truth, nor does it consider the consequences of its selfishness upon society.

Moral relativism is the idea that right vs. wrong is relative to each individual. In other words, each person can determine for himself or herself what is right or what is wrong. It rejects that idea that morality can be determined by an outside entity other than the individual, such as the law, one's parents, or the Bible.

The prevalence of relative morality has caused many people to be reluctant to criticize anybody else's behavior. Sadly, tolerance for other's behavior is now the norm, to the point where behavior that once was forbidden in our society is now accepted and even applauded. The legalization of abortion is just one example among many of the abominable behaviors our culture thinks is normal.

We should point out that moral relativism does have an appropriate place in the Christian walk, for the apostle Paul devotes the entire fourteenth chapter of Romans to this very topic. You may want to study this chapter on your own or with your parents to gain a mature understanding on this important matter. But outside of the boundaries of Romans 14, moral relativism is anti-God to the core.

Think about this question, and see if you can answer it on your own: In what ways does moral relativism foster a false worldview of peace?

The above question has many answers, but common to all of them is this chain of thinking: If no one is wrong, then everybody is right. And if everybody is right, then there is no conflict. And if there is no conflict, then peace is attained. It is a "convenient" conclusion, but it is no more in God's reality than an ostrich that has its head stuck in the sand.

The problem with peace by way of denial is all too evident in the individual who naively thinks all is bliss. The man who spends beyond his means may deny his bank account is in the red, but denial doesn't change his financial state. The man who thinks he is at peace because he has plenty of money is not better off, not unless he has taken the time to seek after God. Such men may think they are at peace, but they do not have the kind of peace offered by Jesus Christ.

Unfortunately, we see it all the time within the family unit: the mother who denies she is spoiling her baby, the father who denies his kids are heading the wrong way, the husband who denies his wife needs his love and security, the wife who denies she is being a nag. The mother or father may think everything is peaceful, but denial does not make it so. The husband or wife may think it better to ignore their marital problems so that "peace" can ensue, but there is tension evident nonetheless.

We have seen it within our society as well: A law may disregard the tension evident between master and slave, allowing the latter to be beaten into compliance, but there is no godly peace for either man. A law may be passed denying the horror of genocide, allowing mothers to kill their unborn babies, but no such mother will be at peace with herself or with her God. A law may turn its head to the example of Sodom and Gomorrah, allowing men to marry men, but there can be no godly peace in such a union. Rather, there is the awaiting wrath of God upon all such laws and the people who support them.

The denial of tension does not result in godly peace. At best, it results in a worldly peace, which is really no peace at all. All of the false worldviews of peace have decisively failed to bring everlasting peace. As we have stated before, no false worldview can properly address the tension between God and man caused by sin.

Of course, unless the issue of sin has been dealt with, there can be no peace. Thanks be to God that a remedy has been provided for us!

True Peace

We opened this lesson with a wonderful quote from Jesus which we will state again, "Peace I leave with you; My peace I give to you; not as the world gives, do I give to you" (John 14:27).

Praise the Lord that He has given us peace!

Peace is the absence of conflict, so how does the peace that Jesus gives remove conflict? His death on the cross erased our sin which was the cause of the conflict between ourselves and God. Jesus willingly and sacrificially shed His blood on the cross for us, and Hebrews 9:22 tells us that "…without shedding of blood there is no forgiveness."

Romans 5:1 tells us the result of man's faith applied toward Jesus' death on the cross: "Therefore having been justified by faith, *we have peace with God* through our Lord Jesus Christ…" (emphasis added).

So Jesus has provided the peace that the world so sorely needs! What a tremendous demonstration of God's love, that "…while we were yet sinners, Christ died for us" (Rom. 5:8). We are no longer enemies of God. Rather, we are His beloved children, born again into His wonderful kingdom!

The One and Only Way to Peace

Notice that true peace of Jesus is not the way of force, nor is it the way of one's own efforts. It is Jesus' way, the way of willful submission to a loving Lord and Master who wants only to love you as His own and to raise you up in the way of His kingdom, the way of righteousness, peace, and joy (Rom. 12:17).

Without faith in Jesus' holy name, no one will ever be able to have true peace. Jesus Himself said, "I am the way, and the truth, and the life; no one comes to the Father, but through Me" (John 14:6).

Jesus also likened Himself as the only door toward peaceful pastures, and He stated that anyone "…who does not enter in by the door into the fold of the sheep, but climbs up some other way, he is a thief and a robber….I am the door; if anyone enters through Me, he shall be saved, and shall go in and out, and find pasture" (John 10:1-10).

Indeed, Jesus is the only way to salvation and true peace. No amount of force, illegal drugs, or wishful thinking can make it otherwise. Only Jesus is the way.

Pass It On!

Jesus said, "Blessed are the peacemakers, for they shall be called sons of God (Matt. 5:9). If you are a son of God who has put his faith in Jesus, then you have the wonderful privilege of being a peacemaker.

Let me tell you something about the importance of this matter. As a son of God, you are far more effective at spreading peace than any of the so-called great men who have tried to promote peace before you without God. You are many times over more effective than the likes of John Lennon or Timothy O'Leary, and you are more effective than even Gandhi or Winston Churchill. These men of great notoriety could not promote real peace because they knew not what it was, for they knew not the Lord Jesus. I would rather hear the way to peace from a six year old who knew Jesus than from an old man who looked elsewhere for his peace.

Jesus has left us with the responsibility of passing His peace on to others. But He has not left us alone. He has given us the power of His Holy Spirit who resides in us. And He has left us with His Holy Word which has much to say in the way of peace. So you are indeed equipped to be a peacemaker, and an effective one at that! Never doubt your ability in this regard.

The Beginning of Peace

In order to be a peacemaker, you must first be at peace yourself. You must have personally put your faith in the Lord Jesus Christ, for in doing so you will have received the peace He has afforded you.

But you must exercise your peace. It will not simply grow without an effort put forth by you. Peace is one of the wonderful fruits of the Holy Spirit (Gal. 5:22), and for fruit to grow it must be fed, cultivated, watered, and otherwise nurtured.

You must also purpose to be a peaceful man. In doing so, you will naturally want others to have the peace that you have enjoyed. Here is some wonderful guidance from Philippians 4:6-9 which shall help you to solidify and enjoy the peace God has given you:

> *Be anxious for nothing, but in everything by prayer and supplication with thanksgiving let your requests be made known to God. And the peace of God, which surpasses all understanding, shall guard your hearts and your minds in Christ Jesus. Finally my brethren, whatever is true,*

whatever is honorable, whatever is lovely, whatever is of good repute, if there is any excellence and if anything worthy of praise, let your mind dwell on these things. The things you have learned and received and heard and seen in me, practice these things; and the God of peace shall be with you.

There is a lot said in the above passage, and you will do well to note both its main and fine points. Let's take some time to consider some of them:

Be Not Anxious

"Be anxious for nothing," says Paul, and so we should heed his good Word. Simply said, you should not be a man who worries. Leave the worrying to scaredy cats who don't know how to put their faith in God. Jesus Himself told us, "Do not be anxious then, saying, 'What shall we eat?' or 'What shall we drink?' or 'With what shall we clothes ourselves?'" God provides food for the birds of the air, said Jesus, so He will do even more so for us! (Matt. 6:24-34).

Trusting in God for all your needs is essential to being a peaceful man. We encourage you to join us in making it a point to live our lives free from worry.

Prayer and Thanksgiving

Paul tells us also to thankfully make our requests known to God. He then said that the peace of God would guard our hearts and minds. Why would our hearts and minds be guarded? I think the key has to do with thanksgiving. If we pray, thanking God for whatever the outcome will be, then we will naturally fall into peace. It's almost impossible to worry when you are truly thankful for your situation, no matter what it is.

Whatever is True....

Consider the things that Paul encourages us to think upon: things that are honorable, lovely, and worthy of praise. Doing so will surely aid you in nurturing peace. I like the fact the Paul does not give us a big long list of specifics in this regard. In his wisdom, he knows that what some people think is lovely, others may not. For example, you might let your mind dwell on a triple olive burger topped with sauerkraut, cooked medium rare and garnished with sardines in hot mustard sauce. On most days, I for one would not find this worthy of praise. You might find honor in shooting your limit of grouse, but your sister may not. Not everyone will think the same way in this regard. But that's okay. God wants us to enjoy and be at peace with whatever we deem excellent.

And while we are to dwell on excellent things, the Bible tells us how we should respond to things that are the opposite, that we should be "...casting down imaginations and every lofty thing raised up against the knowledge of God, and...taking every thought captive to the obedience of Christ" (2 Cor. 10:5). If you want to nurture peace, make sure you train your mind to "cast down" the awful and ugly thoughts that God does not approve of.

"Practice These Things"

Paul tells us to practice the things we have "learned and received and heard and seen" in him. We don't have the privilege of directly hearing and seeing Paul as did the early church, but we most certainly can learn and receive from him. He wrote at least thirteen letters to various churches and people which are recorded in the New Testament, and he was a key figure in the book of Acts. So we have ample opportunity to learn and receive from him, and he assured us that in doing so the peace of God shall be with us.

We encourage you to read often from Paul's letters. Parts of them are easy to understand, and others require interesting study. But you will find peace from what you receive, for you will be reading from a great apostle who knew what he was writing about!

Not a Feeling

There may come a time in your life when you may not "feel" at peace, regardless of the fact that by all indications you are living properly before God. We have even heard of some Christians who doubt their very salvation, simply on the basis that they do not "feel" the peace of God. To be sure, God's peace often is accompanied by a sense of well-being, a sort of tranquility, an inner impression that "everything is okay." But these sensations do not necessarily have to be present to prove you are at peace. Knowing you are at peace, especially with God, is far more an exercise of faith than it is a feeling. Faith is the kind of thing that pleases God. Your feelings, though important, are not essential concerns to Him; neither should they be to you.

We have all heard people say words to the effect that they "felt at peace" about certain matters. If what they mean is that they are exercising their faith and they know God will provide, then we shall say "Amen" to such statements. But if what they really mean is they can now rest because they have pushed all of the nervous jitters out of themselves, then we should be concerned to some degree, for we should not confuse godly peace with some sort of soothing feeling. Nowhere in the Bible is God's peace described in terms of a person being soothed. Such feelings are elusive, and you will be better off not relying on them.

Remember that God's peace is the kind of peace that "passes all understanding" (Phil 4:7). It is not a warm, fuzzy feeling like the one you got from your security blanket when you were a toddler. Nor is it a sense of relief that everything is all right, for relief in this regard implies you have been given a tangible reason not to worry. Neither is peace the sensation of an adrenaline rush which gives you a momentary boost of confidence. Though it passes understanding, perhaps we can at least say that godly peace is the ensuing result of knowing and trusting God. This "result" may involve some kind of feeling, or it may not.

King David continually acknowledged God's peace, but we would be fools to think that he was always calm. When he "walked through the valley of the shadow of death," you can bet that his heart beat hard, and his hand was on his hilt. And yet he had peace, "...For Thou art with me; Thy rod and Thy staff, they comfort me" (Psalm 23). And when Jesus went to the cross, we know that He had peace, for He is the Prince of Peace (Isaiah 9:6). But we know also that He sweat blood.

When facing many of the decisions you will need to make in life, you will do well to remember that peace is not necessarily an absence from all nervous feelings. While you cannot be like the double minded man described by James (1:5-6), you can still contemplate, consider, and even sometimes hesitate, all the while being at peace with God.

Your heart may beat for concern while receiving a kickoff from a band of eleven oncoming guys that want to tackle you flat. Or you may one day start a new job and wonder if you are doing the best thing, but your peace need not be gone. One day you will be watching or waiting nearby as your firstborn son or daughter comes forth into this world. We assure you, you won't be resting calmly by. But will your peace be gone? No sir, not if your trust is in God. Indeed, you will be in countless situations during your life that will involve new and exciting things. In all of these, walk in faith and confidence, knowing that the peace of God will forever guard your heart and mind.

Peace be with you!

Conflict Resolution

There is, to be sure, conflict all around us. Since Cain first murdered Abel, conflict has been the norm. From the bratty toddler who wants his way in the grocery store check out line to the latest crime update on the six o'clock news, tension fills our world. And while we sleep, the tension carries on, for there are wars the world over, both small and large.

In our last study, called "A Lesson on Peace," we discussed how God has made a remedy for conflict and tension. Through Jesus' sacrificial death on the cross, we can have peace with God by faith in His Son. You learned that God desires all of us to be peacemakers (Matt. 5: 9), and that it is largely up to us to bring God's gift of peace to others.

In this study, we will look to see how we can become the best peacemakers that we can be. The Bible has a lot to say on this subject, so we will look to it for our guidance.

Peace, As Far As It is Possible

Before we go further, we want to make something clear, and that is the fact that peace is not always possible. Some Christians get discouraged when they find that not everybody receives the peace that they have to offer. We are not to be discouraged, for the Bible clearly indicates that while we may strive for peace, it may not always be attained: "If possible, so far as it depends on you, be at peace with all men" (Rom. 12:18).

It is apparent, then, that peace is not always possible. God's Word tells us that we are obligated to promote peace as "far as it depends" on us, but there is no guarantee that our efforts will be received.

If you think about it, knowing that peace is not always possible is liberating news. It means that you and I don't have to take the blame if others do not receive our efforts. We can offer our best attempts, but the rest is up to the recipients. To be sure, many will gladly receive our efforts, but others will not. Jesus Himself was not always received, nor were the apostles. If their efforts were sometimes rejected, then so will ours.

So take heart if someone does not want to receive the peace you have to offer him. It's not your fault; it is his. In due time, he may come to his senses, and your prior efforts will have likely helped.

Not If, But When

The Bible is clear that there will be disagreements and even hurt feelings between different people, and Christians are no exception to this rule. In fact, there is something a bit odd about a person if he has lived a fairly long while and has neither offended someone nor been offended (we will learn more about this later on under the heading "Some False Views").

So you are sure to be offended, and you will surely offend others. We can reduce the degree of offenses given and offenses taken, but we will never avoid them all together. The key is approaching the matter as the Bible says we should when offenses are encountered.

As you learn these lessons, keep in mind that they are

primarily given for your own use, for being a peacemaker begins with you. But keep in mind the principles that you learn so that you can, in turn, teach these truths to others.

Communication—Key One

If you are offended or have offended someone else, it is up to *you* to take the initiative to make matters right. Remember, the Bible says "*so far as it depends on you*, be at peace with all men." So you are not to wait for the other person to come to you. This point cannot be overemphasized. Too many people, being either stubborn, shy, or just plain lazy, never seem to understand that peace begins with them.

Taking the initiative involves having a soul-saturated attitude of being a peacemaker. This is true whether you were offended or were the offender. Jesus Himself makes this clear. Let's consider the teachings of the Master:

If You Are Offended....

Jesus said, "And whenever you stand praying, forgive, if you have anything against anyone; so that your Father also who is in heaven may forgive you your transgressions" (Mark 11:25). So you should be quick to forgive anyone who wrongs you, no matter how many times the wrong is committed. Peter once asked Jesus if he should forgive the same person up to seven times. Jesus replied, "I do not say to you, up to seven times, but up to seventy times seven" (Matt. 18:21-22). In other words, don't keep count.

There are those who may take this Scripture to extreme by continually putting themselves in harm's way. But while we are admonished to quickly forgive, we are also called to be careful of being too vulnerable: "Guard your heart with all diligence, for from it flow the springs of life" (Prov. 4:23).

It is not necessary for you or anyone to remain in an abusive relationship. If you are being ruthlessly ridiculed or physically harmed, it is not your obligation to remain a target. While it is our calling to continually forgive, the offender also has an obligation, and that is to repent. Remember, though, that his or her repentance is no guarantee.

If ever you have to remove yourself from a situation, do not feel guilty for doing so, unless of course you are being a crybaby, for we are not to be easily provoked (1 Cor. 13:5). If you must depart, then do so knowing that there are others who need your ministry, and feeling guilty because you were abused simply won't aid your mission.

Guarding your heart does not always mean leaving the scene, although it may. It may mean, simply, to be ready to recognize an attack on your soul or your body. Of course, you do not want to be so on guard that you never trust anybody, so don't go to the extreme by becoming paranoid. Know that "...love believes all things" (1 Cor. 13:7), so you can strike a balance between being on guard and trusting others by exercising the great virtue of love.

If someone asks you for forgiveness, grant it graciously. We are not saying that you need to make light of the matter. In fact, if the matter is a heavy one, let the offender have his say. Both of you will likely benefit from all that is expressed in the way of repentance. If the offender is leaving anything out, it is all right for you to bring it up. But do so in a way so as to restore him. Paul tells us, "Brethren, even if a man is caught in any trespass, you who are spiritual, restore such a one in a spirit of gentleness; each one looking to yourself, lest you too be tempted" (Gal. 6:1).

Go to Your Brother...

There will be times when you are offended and the offender

does not come to you on his own accord. In fact, this may happen more often than not. While this is an inconvenient situation, the Bible tells us that it is up to us to initiate reconciliation. In this regard, you have some choices.

We first counsel you to carefully weigh the matter. While doing so, you will want to exercise *empathy*, which involves the ability to relate to someone by seeing his point of view. Empathy is one of the greater virtues, for from it flow compassion and understanding.

If there is a possibility that the offender doesn't know he has committed an offense, then you should give him the benefit of the doubt in this regard. Perhaps you may determine that the offense is not that big of a deal, and you may opt to do nothing. After all, you do not want to get in the habit of always pointing out an offense committed toward you. Such is the way of whiners and tattle-tales. Your reputation will precede you, and others will think that you are not very fun to be around.

But if the offense is severe enough to really bother you, then you are duty bound to talk to the offender about it. Here's what Jesus has to say about this very matter:

> *And if your brother sins, go and reprove him in private; if he listens to you, you have won your brother. But if he does not listen to you, take one or two more with you, so that by the mouth of two or three witnesses every fact may be confirmed. And if he refuses to listen to them tell it to the church; and if he refuses to listen even to the church, let him be to you as a Gentile and a tax-gatherer.* Matt. 18:15-17

The steps are clear, and you would do well to pay particular attention to the first one, which is to go to him *in private*. Notice that our Lord did not tell us to first complain to our friends about it, nor did he tell us to ignore the matter altogether. This is where many Christians go wrong, yet it is perhaps the most vital step in being a peacemaker.

It does not have to be anyone else's business that you have been sinned against other than the person who committed the sin. By talking to others unnecessarily about it beforehand, you risk jeopardizing the other person's reputation. We are not to bear false witness against anyone, so do not speak ill of a brother until he has a chance to answer your concerns.

If He Listens....

Chances are quite high that you will find a rich reward by going to a brother in private, because he will have listened to you, and you can both move forward in peace. If this is the case, wonderful! Leave the matter at that, and you can both be on your way.

We will not guide you step-by-step on how you can stack the deck in your favor to get an offender to listen to you. Suffice it to say that you will want to exercise a spirit of humility. It is probably best to leave your slingshots, overly ripe tomatoes, and insults at home. But we will suggest a good and proper way to end the conversation, and that is with either a sincere, warm handshake or brotherly hug. You may even want to end the matter in prayer.

You will do well to note that your conversation may not go as expected, but this may not necessarily be a bad thing. You may find, in fact, that the offense was a product of a simple misunderstanding, and that no apology is needed at all. Unless the offense is so blatant that an obvious sin has taken place, you should not convince yourself beforehand that an apology will be required.

If He Does Not...

Of course, there is the chance that the offender will not listen. In this case you are duty bound to present the case before him with another brother. While this may seem burdensome, you must realize that God desires true repentance within the offender and true reconciliation between brothers. Going the distance is an expression of love, though the offender may not initially see your attempt as such. At any rate, you will need to have one or more brothers weigh in on the matter.

Again, we encourage you to go into the conversation with open expectations. The third party may discover a misunderstanding that was not previously known, or you may in fact find out that you were part of the blame. Be humble, and by doing so you will increase the chances of a successful encounter.

How do you bring one or more others into the picture? There is no set formula for this, but you will likely need to brief the others on the matter. If another person is willing, it might be a good idea to let him do most of the talking and confronting.

If Necessary, Take It to the Church

Taking a matter to the church can be a tricky thing. First of all, this assumes that the offender goes to church, for if he doesn't then the matter can pretty much go no further. The matter should be easier if the offender and offended go to the same church, but the offended person should be willing to go the other person's church if necessary. Hopefully, the church involved will recognize the importance of biblical reconciliation. If not, you may find it difficult to take the matter any further.

If You Have Offended....

We must never be so haughty or arrogant that we think we are above sinning against others. The time will come, if it has not several times already, when you will need to attempt reconciliation with someone you have offended.

On this matter, Jesus said, "If therefore you are presenting your offering at the altar, and there remember that your brother has something against you, leave your offering there before the altar, and go your way; first be reconciled to your brother, and then come and present your offering" (Matt. 5:23-24).

If you are a keen reader, you will note that Jesus indicated that reconciliation was more important than even worship before God. God would rather you stop and make things right with a brother than have you tell Him how much you love Him. "Do you love Me?" He asks. "Then get up right now and make things right with your brother."

Do you think it best to wait until tomorrow, or the next day, or the next? If so, you are wrong. Do it immediately, which is God's way. We lament that so many Christians do not practice this essential principle.

Your Parents' Role

The instruction Jesus has given us is most certainly for grown-ups, but we see no reason why it can't apply to young men such as yourself as well. In this regard, seek your parents' counsel every step of the way. If disputes arise between your siblings, your parents will most assuredly want to help you learn how to resolve things. If disputes arise between your friends, your parents will want to be involved. Let them guide you, and chances are great that things will work out well.

Saying Sorry

If you have wronged someone, then admit it. Do so soon, and right away. And while you are at it, offer a sincere, heartfelt apology. While there is no one "right" way on how to do this, you will do well to avoid the phrase, "I'm sorry *if* I offended you, *but...*" The word "if" waters down and practically negates any real admittance that you did anything wrong. It is a wimpy sort of apology, taking no courage at all. The word "but" indicates that you are going to follow up with an excuse. A real man swallows his pride and simply says sincere words to the effect of, "I'm really sorry; I did you wrong. I was insensitive, and I was the fool for being so. Please forgive me." Of course, you need not recite these very words. Offer your own, and in doing so you will be a peacemaker.

Saying sorry involves *repentance*, which means simply that you are not going to repeat your offense. Let the person you have offended know that your wrong behavior will not happen again. The security you offer in this way is a true act of love.

Five False Views

We are obliged to warn you of various ideas that some people embrace that fall short of what God expects from us as peacemakers. These five ideas attempt to promote peace, but they are not really useful for the advancement of true, biblical peace:

False View #1: "It's Always Wrong to Offend"

If you have offended someone but have not sinned, you do not necessarily owe an apology. Nor do you owe it to society to live a life free of offense, for the gospel of Jesus Christ, in part, aims to offend. It aims to bring the sinner to a confrontation with his sin, but in doing so, offers him a way out. Never refrain from sharing the gospel out of fear that you will offend. You are, as Jesus described, a "fisher of man," and there was never one single fish that was netted, snagged, hooked, or speared that did not also take offense in the process.

We are not saying to make it your aim to see how much you

can offend someone. If that were the case, you would be nothing more than an obnoxious noise maker. We are simply saying that there really is no way to offer the good news of salvation to someone without also informing him of his sin. Doing so may likely be offensive. But you will find that some people will be properly offended at their sin, having become aware of it, rather than at you for suggesting something they don't really want to hear. Again, never withhold the gospel for fear of offense.

Neither does God want you to become the sort of person that tries to be so squeaky clean that he never offends someone by what he does. Would God have you apologize to someone for killing a fine eight point buck, simply because the person thought it was wrong to hunt animals? Should a young man apologize for bringing his Bible to public school just because the principal was not pleased? Should a man apologize for voting a certain way because he offended someone by doing do? Heavens, no! But there are so-called Christian men that will try to live in such a way as to always avoid conflict. This is what Jesus referred to, in part, when He said, "Beware when all men speak well of you" (Luke 6:26). Such men are people pleasers, rather than God pleasers. If they are Christians, they are cowardly ones.

False View #2: "I Must Bring Peace to Everyone in My Family"

We have correctly identified peace as being an absence of conflict, and that God desires to be at peace with us, as evidenced by sending His Son, Jesus, to die for our sins. We can say correctly too that God wants His children to live in peaceful harmony one with another (2 Cor. 13:11), and He has given us direction for how to do so in His Word.

But does God expect anything more? This is where many well-meaning Christians go wrong. They strive, and then strive again, to bring peace where it is not welcome. They recognize the conflict between themselves and those who have deaf ears, but they continually press on believing they are forever obligated to do so. They expend their time, their talents, and even their tears to the point of no return. In the name of obligation, they try, and try again, to bring the gospel of peace to those who stubbornly will not receive.

Jesus said, "Do not think that I have come to bring peace on the earth; I did not come to bring peace, but a sword. For I came to set a man against his father, and a daughter against her mother, and a daughter-in-law against her mother-in-law; and a man's enemies will be the members of his household" (Matt. 10:34-36).

On the surface, this may appear to contradict much of what you think you know about true peace. If so, peer in, and understand. Notice Jesus said that He came not to bring peace *on the earth*, meaning in its entirety, for He knew that many would go the way of destruction despite His sacrificial offering of peace upon the cross. He knew that in order to bring peace, He would first have to divide those who wanted peace and those who wanted to reject it, even if it meant that one's family would be divided.

Regrettably, Christians who were raised in unsaved households believe it is their calling to bring their family to repentance, no matter how much pain and time it costs them. It is a wonderful thing if they can, but we should recognize that this is the exception rather than the rule. After all, Jesus said, "A prophet is not without honor except in his home town, and in his own household" (Matt. 13:57).

Indeed, Jesus came to divide. This is consistent with his ministry as a whole. Review Matthew 25:31-32, Luke 12:51, John 7:43, John 9:16, and John 10:19 for just some of the other verses that show that division was a natural result of Jesus' works.

False View #3: It is Wrong to Confront Ungodly Lifestyles or False Doctrines Within the Church

Some Christians erroneously think they are obligated to attempt peace at all costs with those who cause dissention within the Church. Whether it is an occasional attendee or the pastor himself, we are not to tolerate someone who calls himself a Christian but who obviously lives otherwise. The apostle Paul makes this clear in 1 Cor. 5:9-13, especially in regard to immorality, covetousness, idolatry, slander, drunkenness, and swindling. If such people do not repent when they are found out, we are to attempt no further peace with them, for there can be no peace until they repent.

We should point out that the high sin of heresy within a church setting should also not be tolerated. Heresy is a severe departure from sound doctrine. For example, a person in the church who believed and taught that Jesus did not exist before His birth on earth would be committing heresy, and thus would be a heretic. Likewise, a person who believed and taught that Jesus did not really rise from the dead would be a heretic. The Bible tells us how to deal with these kinds of people: "Reject a heretical man after a first and second warning, knowing that such a man is perverted and is sinning, being self-condemned" (Titus 3:10-11).

We see a similar statement by Paul in his letter to the Galatians. The Galatians had been "bewitched" (easily fooled) by a false teacher, and they were beginning to believe in a gospel other than the liberating one Paul taught. In response, he told them, "But even though we, or an angel from heaven, should preach to you a gospel contrary to that which we have preached to you, let him be accursed. As I have said before, so I say again now, if any man is preaching to you a gospel contrary to that which you received, let him be accursed" (8-9).

So we are not to continually attempt to bring peace to

heretics. To be sure, we can offer correction and acknowledge their repentance should they do so, but we are not to pretend they are ministers of God's peace, no matter how angelic or nice they may seem.

False View # 4: The Delusion of Better Days

There are those who think that history suggests a better time somewhere in our past. They long for fairy-tale days when most families and neighbors supposedly lived in harmony. They think along the lines that we are *becoming* corrupt instead of realizing the biblical teaching that mankind without God *has always been* corrupt. But the Bible warns us against thinking along these lines: "Do not say, 'Why is it that the former days were better than these?' For it is not from wisdom that you ask about this" (Eccl. 7:10).

Life was not more peaceful long ago in a little house on the prairie, nor was it during the reign of Queen Anne, nor during the romantic days of Camelot. There are only two kingdoms that now exist: that of the world, and the spiritual one we now reign in with Jesus. The kingdoms of the world have never known peace, for they know not the Prince of Peace. While there may be a nostalgic appeal of days gone by, we should not think of them in terms of better, peaceful times.

False View #5: Anger Always Indicates a Lack of Peace

The Bible is clear on this one, "Be angry, and yet do not sin; do not let the sun go down on your anger" (Eph. 4:26). Being angry is natural, for you have been made in God's image, and the God of love is also a God of wrath.

If you get angry at seeing the various injustices in this world, then take comfort knowing that God does, too. And His Son, Jesus, showed little restraint when the stuffy, religious leaders of the day made a mockery of the temple by converting it into a place of unrighteous commerce. In fact, He turned the tables over and ushered the wrongdoers out with a whip. So the next time you feel as Jesus did, know that your heart beats with His.

Of course, we are not advocating violence as a way of life, for Jesus told us that "...all those who take up the sword shall perish by the sword" (Matt. 26:52). Rather, it is the meek who shall inherit the earth (Matt 5:5). But do not think this is the kind of meekness that suggests you are to be a sissy or even be soft spoken. Jesus was meek, and yet he had none of the traits of a coward. He was a gentle man of tremendous power and self-control, but He used His power for His Father's good work.

But neither are you supposed to be easily angered, for such is the sign of an insecure person. Be angry, and yet sin not. Let the greater virtue of love temper this principle.

A Word on Force

We have indicated that you are not to embrace a lifestyle of violence, but you may be wondering what to do if you are physically attacked. It is not a bad idea to think about this in case it ever happens.

As a young man, you will likely one day join together with a woman of your choosing in holy matrimony. One of your sworn duties and privileges will be to protect your wife and your family from harm. We see no biblical indication to suggest otherwise. What does "protecting" them mean? For certain it means being a man of prayer who shelters his family in the shadow of God's care. Beyond this, we ask that you be the judge if more is needed. We recognize that we live in a world of conflict, and that prayer may not keep us completely immune from it. In all regards, exercise the courage that defines you.

Would you feel badly for stopping a would-be villain dead in his tracks from physically harming your family? I know I would. But I also know this: that I would not feel any more badly for him after he was stopped than I did before he made the foolish decision to attack my family. He was, in reality, already dead before he met me, and his unfortunate encounter with me did not change this fact. It did, however, solidify it. Alas.

What about between now and marriage? What if somebody physically picks on you, your siblings, or even a stranger? I for one am certain that we are not called to ignore it. Nor are we merely supposed to cry for help so as to pass the problem on to someone else (although calling for help may in fact be a very wise thing to do). To be sure, don't use violence as your first means of approach; it is better, if possible, to remove yourself or another from harm's way. But if harm has already come or is on its way, then we do not ask that you stand idly by and become somebody's easy target.

You will, for certain, want to talk with your father about this important matter. You may have further questions, like how far you should go in defending yourself and how you should go about it. You may wonder if it's best to put the attacker's lights out and if you should feel badly about doing so. You may find that your discussion unfolds into even heavier matters, like the rights and wrongs associated with war. Your father will give you the straight shot on all of these important matters.

In all of this, know that you are not to be a vengeful person. Vengeance is the idea that you are going to repay someone for an evil previously done. "Vengeance is Mine," says the Lord. "I will repay…It is a terrifying thing to fall into the hands of the living God" (Hebrews 11:30-31). While it is one thing to deal with violence before or while it happens, it is another to repay evil for evil after the fact. Leave that to God.

In Closing

Many books have been written on the topic of conflict

resolution, and we do not claim to have offered the final word on the matter. Just know that being a peacemaker begins with you, and you are very valuable to God in promoting His kingdom on earth!

Being a Good Steward

Imagine a life where there are no responsibilities. In this world, a boy has no chores, no schoolwork, and no bedtime. He does not have to eat what is put before him, nor does he have to brush his teeth unless he wants to. He can leave his bike out to rust, and he can make his cat fend for his own dinner if he doesn't want to feed it. He can leave his toys lie behind his parents' car, and he can place his dirty laundry wherever his heart desires.

This type of life may appeal to an aimless and slothful boy, but an orderly young man on his way to maturity (which probably best describes you) would cringe at the thought of such a world, for he knows that in the absence of responsibility is the presence of chaos.

A *steward* is someone who manages another's property, finances, or other affairs. You may have not thought about yourself as being a steward, but in reality you are. Everything that you possess has been given to you by God, your parents, or other people. And the things that God or others have given to you are not to be squandered. Rather, they are to be taken care of, and the benefits of doing so are many.

Ownership

We encourage you to embrace a Christian worldview in

regard to ownership, and that is *to consider that nothing you possess is truly yours.* It may appear that your muscles, skin, and hair are your own. The fact that some of your favorite tools and toys have your name on them may indicate they belong to you. It may seem as though the things you have earned by way of work or made by way of your talents are yours. But none of these things are truly yours, for if they were, they would also be *solely yours.*

However, nothing is solely yours, for everything you have was at one time allowed into your possession by God, and we should always remember what our Lord has said to this effect: "I am the vine, you are the branches; he who abides in Me and I in him, he bears much fruit, for *apart from Me you can do nothing.*" (John 15:5, emphasis added). So if you can do nothing apart from God, this must include ownership. If you own something, so does God.

All of It

There are some people who don't want to quite acknowledge that everything they have is jointly owned by God. Some resist this simple truth altogether. Such people are not likely Christians, and so we shouldn't expect them to think otherwise. But there are others, who for whatever reason, acknowledge God but want to think they can have some things to themselves.

Some people believe that God is somehow blessed if they recognize a certain percentage of what He gave to them, but the better way is to simply acknowledge God as the giver of *all* good things (James 1:17). And as we have freely received, so we should freely give (Matt. 10:8). Rather than thinking in terms of how much is yours or how much is God's, we admonish you to consider *everything* as His, for Jesus dwells in you, *and apart from Him you can do nothing.*

If you have something that you are not sure is God's, give it to Him, so that you will have nothing of your own. How do you do this? Simply let it be your sincere heart's desire, and your offering will be done.

If you can get a hold of this view and make it your own, you will go far in protecting yourself and your future family from greed, envy, strife, and a host of other attitudes that will compete for true prosperity and peace. In addition, you will be better able to utilize your strengths and talents and thus be better equipped to love and serve your neighbor. In short, you will be the better man for it.

A Proper Grip

What we are really saying here is that it is useful to have a "proper grip" on the things that you possess. If your attitude is always "Mine, mine!", then your grip is likely too tight. It's all right to get a bit self-centered if you don't want to share your ankle with a shark, but most of the time "mine" is a sure sign of selfishness.

On the other hand, your grip may be too loose if you don't care at all about your talents or the things you possess. If your attitude is usually along the lines of, "I don't care if my gun barrel rusts; it will still shoot okay," or "I can do yesterday's chores tomorrow," or "Somebody else will help the neighbor; I just don't want to," then you are not being responsible with things given to you.

The Brevity of Life

There was a popular bumper sticker a few years back that said, "He who dies with the most toys wins." The drivers who sported this bumper sticker were justifying their desires to stockpile things that would bring them fun and pleasure. Shallow-minded readers thought this saying was cute and funny, but anyone who gave it much thought could easily recognize its depressing conclusion. In time, this bumper sticker gave way to one that attempted to sum the matter up more accurately. It read, "He who dies with the most toys, still dies."

The Bible provides a more thoughtful statement on this matter: "…you do not know what your life will be like tomorrow. You are just a vapor that appears for a little while and then vanishes away" (James 4:14). The psalmist also states, "…Surely every man at his best is a mere breath" (Psalm 39:5).

Perhaps Job had the best attitude toward possessions when he stated succinctly, "Naked I came from my mother's womb, and naked I shall return there" (Job 1:21).

Temporal Treasure vs. Eternal Treasure

Knowing that our life on Earth is but a fraction of eternity is useful, for it helps us to put our possessions and talents into perspective. Life is simply too short to be worried about temporary things. We need to practice the admonishment of the Lord, "Do not lay up for yourselves treasures upon earth, where moth and rust destroy, and where thieves break in and steal. But lay up for yourselves treasures in heaven, where neither moth nor rust destroys and where thieves do not break in or steal, for where your treasure is, there will be your heart also" (Matt. 6:19-21).

This world will often promote the message that the way to riches is through the collection of material things and money. This message will even come by way of religious people. But we admonish you to not believe them. While material goods and money can be a blessing from God, they can also be serious distractions to loving others and doing effective ministry.

King Solomon enjoyed unparalleled wealth at the time of his reign (Eccl. 2:4-9). While he found pleasure in his possessions (10), he nonetheless considered all he had done and all he had owned as a "vanity and striving after wind" with "no profit" (11). He admonished his readers by saying, "Do not weary yourself to gain wealth; cease from your consideration of it" (Prov. 23:4).

So What Does Belong to Us?

Our discussion of stewardship so far has helped us to understand that what we have is God's as much as it is our own. But what exactly do we own? Knowing what we own is essential to knowing how to be a good steward, and so we need to know the answer to this important question.

Toys and Tools

Toys and tools constitute a good portion of the things you own. Some of these are not so easy to categorize, like a slingshot. Is a slingshot a toy, or a tool? It's kind of like a toy in that it is fun to play with, but it is more like a tool in that it is useful in serving certain purposes, like scaring the neighbor's dog when it gets in your trash.

The same holds true for things like hammers and wrenches. Normally these are considered tools, but a case can be made that they are toys because they are fun to work with. Many moms and just as many wives have not been able to tell the difference between a man's toys and his tools. We acknowledge there is little difference.

The point here, however, is discussing the importance of taking care of your toys and tools. So we will get right to the point. Toys and tools cost money (we'll be talking specifically about money in just awhile). The longer your toys and tools last, the better. Simply put: take care of them!

There are few things under the sun that frustrate parents more than having to constantly remind their children to take care of their belongings. If you are the kind of boy who needs constant reminding in this regard, then you would do well to repent and make an about-face.

When you are playing or working with your belongings, have some sense about you. We hope you would have second thoughts about taking your BB gun into the sandbox to bury for safe keeping from pretend Indians. At best, you will cram sand into the seals and other working parts, and at worst you could forget that you buried it and thus ruin it forever. And we hope you would have second thoughts about setting small components to your bike in your uncut lawn. At best, you will take longer to make your repair, and at worst you will lose one or more key parts altogether.

Consider the boy who left his wagon, full of important tools, behind his father's truck all night long in the rain. You might guess what happened when his father left for work in the morning. This unlucky boy was left with only a few tools worth keeping and nothing to tote them in. The father was left with a flat tire and a loose exhaust pipe. A stupid boy concludes that his father should have looked where he was going. The respectful boy recognizes his own foolish error. But the wise and prudent boy stored his belongings in their proper places the night before so as to avoid this scenario altogether.

Know this: Sand and rain are public enemies to most toys and tools. Keep your belongings from these elements, and you will be over halfway to becoming good stewards of them. The other half involves having a "place for everything, and everything in its place."

We offer two final words on the subject of toys, tools, and good stewardship. The first is this: buy, trade, or otherwise obtain the best available tools within your means. There is something to be said for "getting what you pay for." Do your research, and make wise purchases. A tool that costs one and a half times more than a similar tool is usually worth it if it will last twice as long.

The second is this: share your belongings with others. Assume that others will be responsible until shown otherwise. Remember, "Mine, mine" is the way of the selfish and immature. In fact, be glad when you share. Enjoy knowing the recipient is using your belongings. Doing so provides an unmatched blessing.

Collectibles

In our culture, we are conditioned to own a vast array of items. There are many men who have moved their families into larger homes simply to accommodate the accumulation of so many items. This habit of collecting things starts when a man is young. Think about it—if most boys had all the birthday and holiday presents ever given to them placed in a pile, it is doubtful that a full size excavator could fit them all in its bucket.

For the most part, the ability to own and collect things can be a privilege, and so we don't want to make collectibles sound like an evil thing. But we should all pause at the matter occasionally to consider one of Jesus' most probing questions, "For what does it profit a man to gain the whole world, and forfeit his soul?" (Mark 8:36).

Be a good steward of the items you collect. If they are accumulating space, don't assume that more storage room is your answer. It may be that they need a new home elsewhere. But while they are in your possession, take care of them, and be willing to share them appropriately with others.

Special Gifts

From time to time, you may receive a gift that has a special intended meaning from the giver. Your Aunt Mildred may have given you a rare coin that she never wants you to sell, or you may never want to part with the cool pocket knife your grandfather gave you. We encourage you to honor the giver by taking special care of these things, but know that it is impossible to keep anything forever. The day will come when it will be appropriate that you pass these things on to someone else, and in doing so you can honor the spirit in which they were given to you.

Your Clothing

The day will come, if it has not already, when you will be buying your own clothes. It will be then (if that day has not already come), that you fully understand why laundry and the care of apparel was ever made an issue in your home.

We wish there was no need to address this seemingly simple topic, but alas. There is something in the heart of many boys (and some men) which gives reason for many moms (and some wives) to think their sons and husbands purposefully *try* to dirty and even ruin their clothing.

Of course, you and I know this isn't true. From our vantage point, clothes just kind of snag on things and collect dirt by being near it. The matter of remaining snag and dirt-free is simply out of our control.

Whether or not we can maintain a perfect wardrobe will likely remain in the realm of wishful thinking until the Lord comes back. But one thing is certain: you and I can *temper* the degree by which our clothing becomes worthy of the rag-bag. For starters, we can at least attempt to stay dry. In case you haven't noticed, dirt likes to cling to fabric more so when water is involved. The exception may be when soap is added, but we will leave a comprehensive laundry lesson for another day. Simply stated, stay out of the mud, unless of course you must track a wounded animal through it. No one should fault you for this exception.

And there are certain things, to be sure, that you have complete control over. For one, there is simply no reason you have to ever lose an article of clothing. When you are taking off your socks to go after a frog, take note so you don't forget them. The same is true when you shed a coat or shirt because you got too warm. For goodness sake—return home with the same clothes you had when you left!

Another thing: It is almost a certainty that your bedroom has some kind of hamper. If you are a messy boy, it may be that you will have to find yours. Use it for its intended purpose. And if laundry is part of your weekly chores, then keep up on it! A laundry pile is intended to stay small, not for a potential nesting ground for bedbugs or mice.

You and I live in a country where we are blessed to have good clothing at relatively affordable prices. Be a good steward and respect your apparel accordingly.

Money

The Bible speaks about money frequently, and so we need to know a few things about it. Listen carefully, for if you are not the master of money, it will master you.

The Love of Money

For starters, do not love money, for the love of money is the root of all evil (1 Tim. 6:10). Treat money like it is a necessary tool to do certain things, rather than a means by which to gain riches.

However, you will encounter a number of Christians along the course of life who are in fact wealthy. Are these people sinning because of their state? Not necessarily, for the fruit of the Spirit includes self-control. In fact, some of the most respected Christians are wealthy. While there are several warnings in the

Bible about wealth, there is not a single verse that indicates that being wealthy is wrong. In our country, monetary wealth is often the natural consequence of hard work and ingenuity. You, in fact, may become wealthy some day. Just don't make it your life's goal.

By the way, you should know that the overwhelming majority of citizens living in the United States are in fact wealthy in comparison with the rest of the world. Regardless of your family's economic status, never think of yourself as poor.

Avoiding Debt

The Bible admonishes us to not spend more than we make. This is simple, common sense. But in our country, going into debt for non-essential stuff is normal. Resist the temptation to do so. Work on the principle that "cash is king," and you will be better for it.

However, the Bible does not indicate that going into debt is always wrong. It simply says that the "…borrower becomes the lender's slave" (Prov. 22:7). If you do borrow, you should know that you have put yourself into a position where someone (or something, like a bank) may be your master.

In all regards, we admonish you to resist borrowing for depreciable items. Depreciable items are items that go down in value shortly after they are purchased. For example, a new truck costing $25,000 will be worth less than ninety percent of its value after only a couple of days. The same is true for a new bike. If you spend $250 for a new Schwinn, you will be lucky to get even $199 for it the next day. Buying new products is not necessarily a bad idea, but it is usually best to pay cash for them.

Lending

If the Bible cautions against borrowing, then you can bet it has something to say about lending. Indeed it does, for Jesus said, "...lend, expecting nothing in return" (Luke 6:35). So it's all right to loan, but make sure you are really doing the recipient a favor. And it's all right to accept terms for repayment, but just do so with a very loose grip. It is better that your friendship is maintained rather than harmed due to a loan that someone was not able to pay back. In fact, you may want to consider letting the recipient know your intentions and attitude in this regard.

Giving

Of all the things in this lesson, this one is the most important. In short, be a life-long, habitual giver. It has been said many times by wise, godly men that "you can't out-give God." This saying is true. Jesus Himself said, "Give, and it will be given to you. They will pour into your lap a good measure—pressed down, shaken together, and running over. For by your standard of measure it will be measured to you in return" (Luke 6:38).

However, we should warn you about certain religious people who teach that you can "give to get." These people recognize the principle of "give and it will be given," but they practice this principle for the wrong reasons and teach others to do likewise. But you should never give so that you will get. Rather, give because it is an act of love for others.

We encourage you to read the ninth chapter of 2 Corinthians. This chapter wonderfully summarizes the New Testament's attitude and approach toward ministerial giving. It tells us that we should purpose to give often to the needy as we are able, and that we should do so not out of compulsion, but out of a cheerful heart.

Too many Christians are preoccupied with trying to appease

God by giving a certain amount. We encourage you to resist worrying about such matters. Give, and give often, and the rest will take care of itself.

We shall close this topic with an important word of testimony: We have witnessed hundreds of Christians, and we have heard about and read about hundreds of thousands more, who by way of giving to others and trusting God, were *never without* a sufficient degree of food, shelter, clothing, and a few niceties to boot. In fact, the more these Christians gave, the more they had in the way of provisions.

Your House

We do not blame you if up until now you considered the house you live in as something that only your parents owned. But as a young man, you should in fact be thinking of your house in terms of something you also own, rather than simply a place where you hang your hat and store your things.

Your family may either rent or own its home. But in regard to stewardship, the two are the same. If a person rents, he should treat the rented property as though it were his own. So understand that your parents are stewards of the house you live in, and the fact of the matter is *they need your help* in being a good steward of it.

Trust us: you will make your parents proud if you consider yourself as part owner of your house. And don't worry—they won't be charging you rent at this point for simply thinking this way.

Take a good look at your house. It may be a grand piece of work or a humble abode. Regardless, take pride in it. How much pride should you take? If you exercise the same degree of pride as does your father, you will be doing well.

Some boys are afraid of exercising pride in their home because they innately know that they will recognize the work that needs to be done around the place. The truth is that your home needs maintaining regardless of whether or not you take pride in it, so you might as well enjoy it. Pride is an easy thing to capture; it's the kind of thing that likes to stay in you once it is there.

We'll offer a few tips about stewardship and your house: For starters, the outside of your house is the first thing people see. Just as you would not want anyone to see you with a huge spaghetti stain on your chest, neither would you want others to see an unkempt lawn. So keep it trimmed and picked up (this means completely). If large things must be stored outside, line them up neatly in a way that looks orderly from the road.

Also, it will likely be that you will have friends over to either play or work. So think before you do so. Make provisions to hit the baseball *away* from the house, and make sure that not a drop of motor oil gets on your garage floor. Few things discourage a father more than creating unnecessary repairs.

Do you want to increase the degree of respect your parents have toward you? If so, we can offer an almost instant way of doing so, and that is by offering to fix or improve something around the house without being told. If you have not done so before, both you and they will experience a subtle but very real blessing.

This part of our discussion has focused on your house, but you can include the other things in and around your home as being relevant to this topic. Take care of your cars, appliances, and furniture. Treat them as though they were your own.

Other Things

Of course, everything in your possession that you can see,

hear, or otherwise sense is part of your belongings. These are the obvious things, like your clothes, your books, your goldfish, and your piggy bank. But there are other things that you own that you may not normally consider as such. Let's explore some of these:

Your Body

Your body is certainly something in your possession, but it is something that you do not wholly own. The Bible indicates quite clearly that "...your body is a temple of the Holy Spirit who is in you, whom you have from God, and...you are not your own" (1 Cor. 6:18).

What an amazing thing—the Holy Spirit actually *resides in you*! So it should go without saying that we need to be good stewards of our bodies. Appropriately, the Bible places an emphasis on admonishing us to refrain from immoral or impure thoughts and actions (17). Simply stated, God wants us to respect our bodies and use them for good.

There are numerous ways to respect your body, some of which involve the promotion of good health. But be careful, for there are all sorts of faddish ideas about taking super vitamins and avoiding certain kinds of food. Indeed, it seems that there is a new diet offered by the so-called "experts" every week. You will do well to simply listen to the advice of your parents in regard to what you eat. But don't limit the care of your body to food. Make sure you practice good hygiene (including a good bath or shower every other day or so), and get adequate sleep as well. If you are having trouble rising out of bed in the morning, something is probably out of kilter. Figure out what is wrong and make proper remedy.

We assume that you already know to avoid distractive habits—like cracking your knuckles or peeling away scabs. At best these only serve as irritations for others to see, and at worst they may be causing undesirable, long term side effects.

As a young man near or in his teens, we probably don't have to encourage you to stay physically fit. It is likely that you are already interested in some kind of physical activity like lifting weights or jogging. While activities like these are useful, we admonish you to embrace a lifestyle that makes physical activity commonplace. Work hard around your home and for others, and learn at least a few basic trade-related skills.

You may also want to take up an individual hobby or sport like swimming, rock climbing, or hunting. In all regards, explore the great outdoors, and your body, soul, and spirit will all be the better for it! But in all of this, know that your body is the house of God. Respect and treat it accordingly.

In our estimation, the best means of stewardship of our bodies is to follow this wonderful biblical admonishment: "I urge you therefore, brethren, by the mercies of God, to present your bodies a living and holy sacrifice, acceptable to God, which is your spiritual service of worship" (Rom. 12:1).

Indeed, there is a wonderful, beautiful ease to worshipping God, and that is to simply offer your body to Him. How do you do this? By having the simple attitude which says, "Here I am, Lord; from my head to my toes, have Your way with me...."

Your Talents

Everyone has certain skills, and you are no exception! As you know by now, these skills are co-owned by God, for He is the one who enables you to work and to express your skills.

So what are you going to do with your talents? The answer should be plain, but too many people don't even consider the question. In short, you must use your talents for good.

What does using your talents for good mean? It means keeping a humble spirit about yourself and what you are able to do. Don't be too much of a show-off (except toward your mother—you can probably never show off too much to her). And your talents, as they are used, should in some way better your fellow man.

Perhaps the matter of talents can be summed up by Paul's admonishment, "Whatever you do in word or deed, do all in the name of the Lord Jesus, giving thanks through Him to God the Father" (Col. 3:17). "In the name of the Lord," means you are representing Him, so do so accordingly.

The Fruit of the Spirit

In an upcoming lesson, you will learn a good deal about the fruit of the Holy Spirit. You probably already know a few things about it, and so we should discuss this topic in light of stewardship.

As you know, the Holy Spirit resides in you. But He doesn't do so just to "hang out." He does so to guide you, convict you, and to have fellowship with you. And in doing so, He intends to grow and "bear fruit" in your character. Galatians 5:22-23 describes the fruit of the Holy Spirit as love, joy, peace, patience, kindness, goodness, faithfulness, gentleness, and self-control.

As it develops, this fruit comes into your possession, and you are to be a steward of it. Beautiful, ripe fruit is not meant to be stored in a hot, musty warehouse. No, it is to be available for the delight and betterment of others.

Be proud of the Lord and thankful to Him for developing a fruitful character within you. Doing so is an act of stewardship in its own right. And proper pride and thankfulness will allow Him to bear the fruit even more.

Your Potential

No man could be a good steward of his potential if he didn't know he had it. What is "potential?" Your potential is *your capability to do things*, even when you aren't doing them. Just as a match has the potential to start a fire, so you also have the potential to do certain things.

Do you recall our lesson entitled "Being Strong and Courageous"? If so, you know that as a Christian, you wield a great and wonderful strength. Part of being a steward of this strength is having a constant, never-ending awareness that this strength is yours. Even when you seem weak, you have an amazing potential to exercise God's power that is within you. Here are some key Bible verses that will help you to understand this vital concept:

> *...you shall receive power when the Holy Spirit has come upon you...*   *Acts 1:8*

> *I can do all things through Him who strengthens me.*   *Phil. 4:13*

> *...I have written to you, young men, because you are strong, and the word of God abides in you, and you have overcome the evil one.*   *1 John 2:14*

> *"...greater is He who is in you than he who is in the world."*   *1 John 4:4*

To be sure, you have tremendous potential—potential to learn, grow, love, and exercise power. Be a good steward of your potential by always recognizing you have it so that you can use it when the time is needed.

Time

Time is a very valuable and precious commodity. If you lose a sock, you can buy a new one or bribe your sister to knit you a replacement. If you lose your piggy bank, you can go to work to replenish its contents. But you can never get back even one second of your life.

It is no wonder the Bible admonishes us to "…be careful how you walk, not as unwise, but as wise, making the most of your time, because the days are evil" (Eph. 5:15-16).

So, being a good steward involves using your time wisely. Seize opportunities to accomplish whatever is at hand, and make opportunities when there are none to be found.

Heirs With Christ

Being a good steward involves using wisely all that is in your possession. So far we have explored some of the obvious and some of the not-so-obvious things. We will now go one step further into the not-so-obvious:

The Bible declares that as sons of God, we are *heirs* with Christ (Romans 8:17, Eph. 3:6). An heir, if you do not already know, is someone who inherits something, usually by way of someone else's death. If we have inherited everything that Jesus has, then we have much in our possession that we are responsible for. We make mention of this not to overwhelm you, but rather so you know what is in your possession. If Jesus owns it, so do we!

While some Christians get excited about owning the earth and all that is in it, there is something even more exciting in the way of being an heir with Christ. Perhaps this can best be summarized by Peter's revelation to us: "… His divine power has granted to us everything pertaining to life and godliness, through the true knowledge of Him who called us by His own glory and excellence" (2 Peter 1:3).

Let that sink in for a moment. And after it sinks in, let it stay there. You have *everything pertaining to life and godliness*! That pretty much sums up all you will ever need. Let your prayer be that you will know how to be a good steward of it.

The High Calling

You now know what you possess, and you know the importance of being a good steward of it all. So it is appropriate to leave you with this pointed admonishment:

You *must* be a good steward. You cannot afford to be lax about this. Neither can you shirk from fear. You would do well as a follow up of this lesson to read the parable of the talents in Matthew 25:14-30. You will see there the truth that God puts things into your possession so that in the end, you will give back to Him an increase. While this is an awesome responsibility, we know it is one that you are equipped to handle. In fact, it is the way of blessing for yourself, for others, and for God who is the giver of all good things.

So we admonish you in the name of the Lord: Be wise with all that you have all the days of your life!

Made for Marriage

The subject of marriage is one that we are most proud of. How privileged we are to present to you some of what we know about it!

If you are new to Teleo Scouts, you would do well to first read our previous lesson entitled "Treating Ladies Properly." Those who have already studied this lesson might benefit from a review. Indeed, "Treating Ladies Properly" and "Made for Marriage" go hand in hand as much as any two lessons can.

You will find, in the lesson that follows, encouragement upon encouragement regarding this wonderful topic. To be sure, we will include cautions, but each point made will guide you toward truth, wisdom, and sound reason.

In the Beginning...

As you know, God created the world and all that is in it. But did you know that when He did so He also created the first *institution*, and that this institution was marriage? This fact is wonderfully laid out for us in Genesis, and it is one of the most revealing narratives of God's intention for intimacy ever written:

The Lord God formed man of dust from the ground, and

breathed into his nostrils the breath of life; and man became a living being...Then the Lord God took man and put him into the garden of Eden to cultivate it and keep it...

Then the Lord God said, "It is not good for the man to be alone; I will make him a helper suitable for him."...So the Lord God caused a deep sleep to fall upon the man, and he slept; then He took one of his ribs, and closed up the flesh at that place. And the Lord God fashioned into a woman the rib which He had taken from the man, and brought her to the man.

And the man said, "This is now bone of my bones, and flesh of my flesh; she shall be called Woman, because she was taken out of Man."

For this cause a man shall leave his father and his mother, and shall cleave to his wife, and they shall become one flesh. Gen. 2:15, 18, 21-24

God Ordained

When we say that marriage was the first institution, we are stating that it was purposefully put into place by someone. The Genesis narrative makes it clear that this Someone was God. Indeed, He is the one who created and ordained it. That is why some people refer to marriage as *holy matrimony*.

There are those who do not want to acknowledge that God created marriage, for if they acknowledged Him, they would also have to be accountable to Him. Instead of believing marriage was God ordained, they have convinced themselves that marriage is a *social construct*, meaning that certain societies long ago "invented" marriage to suit the needs of their culture.

But marriage is not something invented by man. How

foolish to think this were even possible! Man could not have invented the institution of marriage any more than he could have spoken himself into existence. On the contrary, marriage is a heavenly construct, and as sure as the heavens reflect the glory of its Maker, matrimony is "clad in the beauty of a thousand stars."

Marriage—A Perfect Design

Could a man improve upon the splendor of the heavens by tossing tinsel in the sky? Of course not; so neither could he hope to improve upon God's design of holy matrimony. From the beginning, the institution of marriage was a perfect one. And within His design, there are clear qualities which comprise this perfection. Let's discuss some of these now:

One Man and a Wife

Marriage, as God has intended, is the holy union between a man and a wife. One would think that this quality would be self-evident, but unfortunately this is not always so. In fact, certain adherents to worldly ideals have made a downright mockery of holy matrimony. In this regard, they have attempted to redefine marriage altogether. This mockery has resulted in a variety of expressed ideas, ranging from the ridiculous to the grotesque.

We do not want to spend too much time describing what marriage is not. Sufficient to say, marriage is between a man and a wife, nothing less. Suggesting that it could be anything less would be like comparing the Grand Tetons to a termite hill, or the Pacific Ocean to a mud puddle, or the Great Plains to a briar patch. You get the idea. One simply cannot take the majestic and make from it the mundane.

A Lifelong Commitment

There are some who have concluded, for selfish reasons, that a man and woman can just live together as long as it conveniences them to do so, instead of honoring God's original intention. Not surprisingly, God's intention involves a *lifelong commitment*.

Some religious leaders once asked Jesus a question related to this topic:

> *And some Pharisees came to Him, testing Him, and saying, "Is it lawful for a man to divorce his wife for any cause at all?" And He answered and said, "Have you not read, that He who created them from the beginning made them male and female, and said, 'For this cause a man shall leave his father and mother, and shall cleave to his wife; and the two shall become one flesh'? Consequently they are no longer two, but one flesh. What therefore God has joined together, let no man separate."*
> *Matt. 19:3-6*

There are a number of important things that we can gather from this passage. For starters, we note that Jesus Himself, when posed a question, went to the Scriptures to present His answer, for He knew that Holy Scripture is the supreme authority on all matters. This is true not only for the subject of marriage, but for all other subjects as well.

Another key point is Jesus' emphasis that a man and woman become *one flesh* upon the marriage union. This is a vital component to your full understanding of the matter. One day you will likely be married, and you must understand that you and this lucky lady (although you may be the luckier), will no longer be considered two people in God's eyes. Rather, you will be one.

This passage also emphasizes the importance of honoring commitment. Jesus said that no man should attempt to separate what God has joined together. Just as God has merged the ocean with the shoreline and the forest with the field, so too has He joined man and woman through holy matrimony. The two are as inseparable as can possibly be.

Oh, how we lament that not all who are joined in holy matrimony understand the strength of their bonds! Perhaps you, like us, have been witness to the awfulness of divorce. Divorce is never ideal. At its worst there are casualties, and at its best there is an awful state of confusion one must recover from, like waking from a horrible dream yet thinking you are still caught in it.

We will say a final word on the subject of divorce and then be done with it. Simply stated, you must purpose that divorce will *never* be an option for you to initiate.

Love and Commitment

We are proud to report that we have been witness to thousands of blessed, rich, and wonderful marriages. And we know that there are millions more than those we have witnessed. What accounts for the success of these marvelous relationships? To be sure, there are several contributing factors, but central to them all is an understanding of the relationship between love and commitment.

Perhaps no greater passage describing the essence of true love can be found than the thirteenth chapter of 1 Corinthians. In part, it says...

> *Love is patient, love is kind and is not jealous; love does not brag and is not arrogant, does not act unbecomingly; it does not seek its own, is not provoked, does not take into account a wrong suffered, does not rejoice in unrighteousness, but rejoices with the truth; bears all things, believes all things, hopes all things, endures all things. Love never fails....*

While we can glean several things from this wonderful passage, one thing seems to stand out. If you consider the various phrases used to describe love, you will notice that *not one of them suggests that love is an emotional feeling.* So we can see that love is a commitment more so than anything else.

How does one exercise patience? By *choosing* to do so. How does one exercise kindness? By *choosing* to do so. How does one exercise belief, hope, or anything else that comprises love? The answer is always the same—by *choosing* to do so. Perhaps no other thing that you have learned in Teleo Scouts is as important as the conclusion that you will find here, and that is that *love is a choice, rather than a feeling.* If you are to be married one day, you will do well to dwell on this truth.

How does one choose to love? By commitment toward this purpose. So you can instill the important virtue of commitment toward your future wife now, even though you may not yet know her face or name. You can do so by thinking of her and praying for her, all in a spirit of awe, commitment, and anticipation.

To what degree should you love your wife? The love you express for your wife should be greater than your love for anything else. In fact, the measure of your love for your wife should be proportional to the love that Christ has for His church. Ephesians 5:25 says, "Husbands, love your wives, just as Christ also loved the church and gave Himself up for her." So your love will need to be a *sacrificial one.*

Sacrificial Love

What is sacrificial love? Among other things, it involves a willingness on your part to become lesser so that your wife can become greater. It also involves accepting her for who she is, rather than trying to make her become something worthy of your acceptance. After all, does Jesus make a person behave perfectly before He will accept him or her? Of course not (although there are plenty of religious people who would suggest otherwise).

You will see plenty of men getting angry at their wives for trivial things, but we implore you not to follow their ways. Getting mad for simple matters is really a waste of everybody's time and energy, and we would like to spare you (and others) of this. To the degree that Jesus tolerates your behavior, you should tolerate your wife's, and always give her the benefit of the doubt in this regard. In doing so, remember that "love is patient, love is kind...." Emulate Jesus, and you will do right.

We should know that sacrificial love can be taken to an extreme not intended by God. We have witnessed plenty of men who let their wives have their ways in just about everything. Perhaps these men think they are somehow demonstrating sacrificial love, but more often than not they are likely just "giving in" to avoid a fight, or they may not know any other way. Some of these men, though they may be aware of their calling to lead, are nonetheless ill-equipped to do so.

Leadership and You

Simply stated, you are to lead your wife and the rest of your family as God gives increase. The Bible says, "For the husband is the head of the wife, even as Christ is the head of the church: and He is the savior of the body" (Eph. 5:23).

Does this mean that you will simply declare the marching orders and your wife will follow suit? Not exactly, although your leadership may in fact need to be direct at times. But just as often as not, you will be leading by being a *servant* to her.

God often allows us to make decisions simply because He wants to fulfill the desires of our hearts (Psalm 20:4). Likewise, you should want to serve your wife by granting her desires. Of course, God does not always give us everything we want, and so you will need to discern God's will in regard to her desires. But when in doubt, listen and respond accordingly to her. If you have a wife who loves the Lord, you will be wise in understanding that she will often be able to discern God's will in ways that you cannot.

Of course, leadership as a husband involves more than interaction with your wife. It involves an understanding that the various responsibilities of decision making rest on your shoulders and a willingness to live up to this calling. The good news, as you likely know, is that *you were made for this purpose.* We have no doubt in our minds that you can meet or exceed all expectations in this regard.

It is our view that the wisest and most efficient means for a man to provide for his family is for his labor to be the primary means of income for the family. In fact, it is our conviction that he should make enough money to meet the family's budget without his wife having to work. Are we saying it is wrong for a wife to work for income? By no means! We just think it is usually best if the family does not have to *depend* upon her income. We hope you follow our advice in this regard. Needless to say, you will have to be a good, steady worker.

It will also be up to you to set various policies in your home. Where will you live and what kind of house will you live in? Who will pay the bills, and who will be in charge of cleaning? What kind of vehicle will you buy? Will you have a garden? Of course, these decisions and many others will need to be made with your bride in mind. You will want to seek her insight, her desires, and her counsel. Together you can make these decisions. But the responsibility of the whole matter rests on you.

We will offer two cautions in regard to the leadership you will one day exercise as a husband. The first caution is to not take the calling of your leadership to an extreme. It seems there are always a few so-called men who think that leading their wives means controlling them in some way. We have seen certain men become so arrogant in this regard that they make their wives follow them around, rarely letting them speak for fear of losing public respect. How sad this is. It is as though these men were teased on the playground during grammar school and are now trying to make up for their insecurities by oppressing their wives. You shall have no part of this nonsense.

However, there are those men that do not take their calling to lead seriously enough. These men will let their wives overspend, over-plan, over-direct, and over-lead in all manner of daily living without bringing a balance to the order of things. Some of these men may be victims of overly assertive women, but we wonder how many of these women are overly assertive simply because their husbands won't lead. This is a common trap that many couples fall into, and the consequences often trickle down to the children who are never sure of the family's order.

Planning Your Marriage

"Wait a minute!" you protest. "I'm only halfway through this lesson and you already want to plan my marriage. I'm not ready...Slow down!"

Relax, we are not wanting to determine what kind of cake you will be having or whether or not your wedding will be held indoors or outdoors (although we do recommend a splendid pig roast with all the fixings). What we mean by "planning your marriage" is thinking about your wife now, even though you may not have yet met her. If this seems odd, hear us out....

Too many couples never give a thought to marriage before they tie the knot. In fact, there are those who literally elope and get married within an hour of deciding to do so. While some of these foolish couples may be spared their due folly, more often than not they will somehow pay for their lack of preparation. Indeed, they would have been better off to study the concept of marriage beforehand.

Do Not Be Unequally Yoked

What kind of woman will you marry someday? We hope you have some ideas founded in wisdom, but if you don't, we will be glad to offer a few. For one, we admonish you to marry a lady who loves the Lord as much as you do. It will be acceptable if she loves Him more than you do, as long as you don't argue about this in public.

Do you love the outdoors? If so, would you marry someone who spends her day under the bed? Do you love fine food? If so, would you marry someone who would rather eat cardboard than steak? If you loved dogs, would you marry someone who preferred the company of fleas? Of course not! Why then, would you ever think of marrying a non-Christian who, at the core of her very soul, was opposed to everything you knew to be right and true?

The Bible offers clear direction on this matter: "Be ye not unequally yoked together with unbelievers: for what fellowship hath righteousness with unrighteousness? And what communion hath light with darkness?" (2 Cor. 6:14, KJV).

A "yoke," in case you don't know, is a wooden bar or frame by which two draft animals (like horses or oxen) are joined at the heads or necks for working together. If this team of two animals are "unequally yoked," they will not be able to travel in a straight line, for one will be strong and the other weak. At best, they will wander off the intended course many times. At worst, they will go in many circles and be forever lost. God wants neither; rather, He wants you to marry a lady who is as spiritually strong as He intends you to be, so that you can work together in a straight line toward the place of His leading.

So picture yourself as a strong and able ox, and behind you is the master of the field and the plow which you are honored to pull. But yoked alongside you is a droopy-eyed basset hound whose feet don't come anywhere close to reaching the ground. And every time a rabbit or chipmunk comes in sight, this hound sounds off and tries to shake himself free.

We wouldn't blame you if the thought of being teamed up in this way took the spunk out of you. Yet this is kind of what it would be like if you were unequally yoked to a non-believer in marriage.

Role Models

If you have been blessed to be raised in a godly home, then you likely need to look no further than your own mother as a wifely role model. Is your mother perfect in this regard? Probably not (although she may be), but you should consider and appreciate everything and all that she does in the way of being a godly wife to your father, and look for a woman one day that will be somehow like her. Of course, you will find enough variance within the similarities to keep you on your toes. But you will be a blessed man if your wife is like your mother in at least a few ways.

Consider also some of your mother's friends. It's probable that you have already seen godly character emulated from these women. Mark these qualities down, and make it a point to determine a pattern in the things you appreciate.

Consider too the godly qualities that you see in your sisters or your sisters' friends. Now we realize that there may be a few things about some of these girls that are downright turn-offs. Maybe one of your sisters leaves her hairbrush on the vanity counter every morning. Maybe her friend talks too much or voices disapproval when you get blood on your pocketknife. But we aren't talking about these things. Rather, we are talking about virtues. Learn how to recognize and appreciate virtues. The importance of this matter deserves special attention, and so we will discuss it further now.

Above All Else—Virtue

In short, make virtue the supreme target of your affections. More than money, appearance, fashion, or fame, be attracted to virtue. Is she kind? If so, good. If not, then remove her from consideration. Is she patient? If so, good. If not, avoid consideration of her. And so on.... Let the list of heaven's great virtues be your compass toward a godly wife. Remember, "If virtue accompany it... it is the heart's paradise."

There are those who may think your standards are too high by measuring a lady against godly virtue. But on what grounds should you lower your standards? On the contrary, we say *raise* your standards when in doubt, for we know you will not be able to raise them past the highest heavens, and the highest heavens are where the truly virtuous reside.

What do you say to "good looks"? Do you place a demand on this vain commodity? If so, we admonish you to consider otherwise, for the appearance of a lady, unlike her virtue, can be stolen by either time or travesty. And we have yet to meet a married man, who upon exercising true, sacrificial love, did not consider his bride as the supreme measure of all true beauty. Let the love of virtue guide your heart, and the concern of physical affairs will take care of itself.

Recognizing Virtue

How will you know virtue? Virtue is almost impossible *not* to recognize. If you do not recognize it, it is either because it is not there or you fell asleep during your study of the matter.

Virtue comprises the *persona* of a lady, and so you will see it manifest, among other ways, upon her countenance. She will have the kind of smile that is never forced, and her candor will be smooth and confident, like the Spirit who resides within her. As her friend, she will make you proud for knowing her. As your wife, she will empower you beyond measure.

Recognizing virtue sometimes involves having a "blind eye" to the things that might otherwise distract a fussy man. In this regard, consider how Christ views His bride. Does He see His bride (the church) with faults, or does He see his bride as being holy, pure, and perfect because He has made her to be so? The answer, of course, is the latter.

Therefore, as Christ sees his bride as pure and perfect, so should you also see your bride. View her as Christ views her, and you will see virtue upon virtue. You may, in fact, see virtue where others don't, but remember, reality is always from God's perspective.

Virtue and You

So far we have stated quite a bit about the importance of virtue within your bride-to-be. But what about your own virtue? Should you expect this wonderful lady to want to marry a man who cannot demonstrate the same qualities that he expects from her? If she is virtuous, she is likely wise, and so you should expect her to have a standard that is as high as your own.

Do you consider yourself "a catch" for a lady someday? If not, are you on your way to becoming one? We trust you are. And know this—that it is okay for you to see yourself as a catch, for you must be confident that you have something good to offer your bride-to-be. Just don't let your estimation of yourself get so big that it clouds reality or makes you haughty.

What kind of man will you be toward your bride-to-be? Will you guard her dignity, her character, and her purity? We trust you will. She is, after all, the daughter of the Most High, and so treat her accordingly. Even though you may not have yet met her, think of her kindly with godly anticipation. So guard your own dignity, your character, and your purity. And do so in both thought and deed.

Where Is She?

All this talk about high standards may have you thinking that the virtuous woman we have described doesn't exist. After all, "An excellent wife, who can find?" (Prov. 31:10). Rest assured, she does exist, and it will be your privilege to find her. The good news is that the search will be somewhat easier than you think, for in all likelihood she will want to be found.

But how will you recognize her? In our estimation, this is a question that has paralyzed too many Christian young men. There seems to be a teaching that suggests that there is only one woman whom God has predestined to be your wife. However, we find this teaching to be against sound, biblical reason. The Bible indicates clearly that "He *who finds a wife* finds a good thing and obtains favor from the Lord" (Prov. 18:22, emphasis added). God has equipped you with wisdom and insight in this regard, and He allows you the freedom to find and select a wife who is suitable for you.

Of course, talking about finding a wife assumes one thing, and that is that you are ready to find a wife. Some of you reading this lesson are far more interested in making tree forts and go-carts than you are in girls, and we do not ever wish to diminish the importance of these things. And we know that most of our older readers, those in their later teens, are likewise not quite ready to go wife-shopping. We are not discussing this matter to accelerate it; it's just that we know that time has a way of slipping by. It is inevitable that you will one day be attracted by God's greatest design, and so you must have certain convictions on the matter which will set you up for success.

The Road to Marriage

We will state up-front that we do not believe the Bible has a dyed-in-the-wool formula for how a young man should meet a lady and eventually select her for a wife. But neither is the Bible silent on this matter. On the contrary, it offers universal truths that speak to us, truths rich in wisdom.

One of the most vital admonishments offered in Scripture is Proverbs 4:23: "Watch over your heart with all diligence, for from it flow the springs of life." This proverb acknowledges what we already know, that the heart is something vulnerable, subject to damage, and that we must protect it.

The Dangers of Dating

The need to protect our hearts is why we are so very much opposed to the conventional dating system that is prevalent in our culture. Think about it—dating actually *purposes* to promote affection (often quite deeply), and while doing so offers no *defined end-in-mind*.

Ask any proponent of dating what the ultimate purpose is, and he or she will tell you words to the effect "to have a good time," or "to learn how to act in the presence of the opposite gender," or "to accumulate multiple experiences." While all of these purposes have varying degrees of validity, they can all easily be accomplished in richer, safer, and more efficient ways, ways that do not require the need to expose or share one's heart.

The typical dating process goes something like this: A young man or lady (sometimes barely teen-aged) is physically attracted to someone (who is equally young and naïve). Having hardly thought the matter out, they exchange some sort of mutual affection. "I like you more than anybody else," "You are always on my mind," or "I love you" are just some of the many things that might be said, written, or otherwise implied. And once an expression is received in the heart of another, there is left a looming, unanswered question: *"For how long* will you like me more than anybody else?", "*For how long* will I always be on your mind?", "*For how long* will you love me?"

Thus, there is always an ongoing uncertainty which is never really satisfied. And of course, there *is* an answer to the question "for how long," which is inevitably revealed. This answer, unfortunately, is something similar to, "*I will demonstrate fondness, think about, or otherwise love you until I become tired of you or determine that you are no longer worthy of my affection, at which point I will attempt to return your heart, if in fact I am still able to present it in one piece.*"

The irony of the dating system is that it *practices breaking up*! By the time some men and women think they are ready to get married, they will have already been in dozens of relationships with varying degrees of intimacy, each of which resulted in a break-up. Sadly, a pattern emerges in which a person *expects* a relationship to go sour. It is human nature to think thus. Really, it is no wonder so many marriages end in divorce. In reality, dating has contributed to divorce by conditioning our culture to think that breaking up is a normal thing.

So, are we against the idea of you or other young men spending time with certain ladies? By no means! We would not deprive you of experiencing the presence of God's crowning achievement. But we do know that your journey to marriage presents the opportunity for you to embrace certain convictions that will set you and your bride-to-be up for success.

Courtship

Much has been written about the subject of courtship, and we do not claim to have the final word on the matter. Nor do we claim that there is any one-set-way of engaging in the courtship process. The Bible does not claim to present one, and so neither do we. So what we offer here are some simple, straightforward principles that can guide any man (and his bride-to-be) toward the beginnings of a successful marriage:

Know How to Recognize Her

First and foremost: Know what you are looking for in a future wife. We have already discussed the importance of virtue, so confidently assess what is important to you. Discuss these matters with your parents or close friends. While it's not vital, it may be useful to write these qualities down.

Proponents of dating argue that there is no way of really knowing a lady unless you date her. Respectfully, we disagree. We see little to be gained and lots to be lost with this approach. What adherents to the dating view fail to realize is that the best way to *really* know a lady is by observing her in *real life situations*. If a man is formally dating a lady, there is always the temptation to perform in certain ways to gain approval.

A far better way is to observe and study how a lady behaves toward her parents, her siblings, her friends, strangers, and of course, you. And the best places to make these observations are in natural ones, ones that are not contrived and where there is no need to wonder about ulterior motives. In making your observations, consider a lady's convictions on important matters and how they are naturally manifested in her life. Meanwhile, enjoy her company!

Seeking Godly Wisdom

The book of James tells us that "...if any of you lacks wisdom, let him ask of God, who gives to all generously and without reproach, and it will be given to him" (1:5). Without the seeking of Godly wisdom in all matters (especially this one), you are like a traveler going out in a stormy forest at night without a compass. Seek God's input on whom you are to marry, and you will be richly rewarded.

Parental Input

We strongly suggest having a conversation with your parents in regard to when you might be ready to formally pursue marriage. There are several variables to consider, like your age, how much money you might want to have saved up, or how far along you might be in your schooling or career. The Bible offers no rules or formulas to these things, and so we will not imply any.

Of course, never feel pressured to get married. There is nothing implied in this lesson that suggests you should start your search now. That being said, we will offer some guidelines in regard to the timing aspect of this whole thing.

When you become fond of a particular lady, let your parents know. Get their wisdom and insight on the matter. But it is important that your feelings *not* be shared with the lady, at least not quite yet. In fact, we implore you to keep your thoughts only to yourself, your parents, or an appropriate mentor. While there is wisdom in the counsel of many, there is also foolishness in prematurely broadcasting something.

If, in due time, you feel you are ready to pursue this lady with the intent to marry, then approach your parents and make your case! Don't worry—they won't be shocked, not if you have kept them informed. Besides, in many ways they know you better than you know yourself. They know this day is coming.

Regardless of your parents' reaction, honor it, especially if you are under their roof. Once you are grown and on your own, you will have the right and obligation to do whatever God has laid on your heart. But while under your parents' domain, their word should be revered and respected. If there are concerns or objections voiced by your parents, listen intently. It may be that they see something clearly where you do not. If you want to make an appeal, do so in a spirit that promotes mutual respect.

Remember, your parents love you and want what is best for you. If this was true for baths and bedtimes when you were younger, how much more will they want your marriage to be a success! And keep in mind that they are not losing a son so much as they are gaining a daughter-in-law. You will do well to hear their entire heart on the matter.

The Next Step

Let's assume your parents wholeheartedly applaud your intentions. Now what? We suggest that you don't order your tuxedo quite yet. We advise you next to discuss the matter with the lady's father. Don't worry, if he has any wits about him, he won't be caught off-guard. Approaching him will be a gesture that he will surely appreciate. Remember, just as your parents will be gaining a daughter-in-law, so will your bride's father be gaining a son-in-law. So you should be treating this man as though he were your own father.

By now you have probably gotten the picture that this is serious stuff. Of course it is! But this whole process can be one of the most blessed experiences of your life. Approach this opportunity accordingly.

Keep in mind that you are not at this time asking permission to propose. You are asking permission to court the lady, to formalize and define the relationship as something that intends to go toward marriage.

How do you approach your potential father-in-law? We encourage you to do so confidently. While there is to be expected a certain degree of nervousness, you should not act as though you were a stray dog about to get yelled at for walking onto the lawn. If you are really nervous, it may be that you have good reason to be. Do you anticipate objections? If so, are the objections legitimate ones? You should be ready to address any and all concerns that might arise. Have the same heart that

186 • Made for Manhood

Jacob had when he first addressed Rachel's father, and you will be just fine (Gen. 29).

But what exactly should you say? We're not at liberty to tell you what to say anymore than we would tell the President what to say in his Inaugural Address. But if you really need a starting point, you can try something like, "Mr. Dowry (or whatever his name really is), I want to talk to you about Princess Flowerpetal (or whatever her name really is). I want to hear your thoughts about my desire to get to know her better. I'm really impressed with her and would like to tell her how I feel. My parents approve of my desire, and I thought it would be important to talk with you next."

Something along the lines of our suggestion would be appropriate, but we acknowledge that you could probably offer something much better. Just be yourself, and the rest will take care of itself. The whole heart of the matter is to let the lady's father know that you value him and have his best interests in mind.

What Says She?

It may be that the lady's father or mother will want to talk to their daughter about this matter before anything goes further, or it may be that her father wants you to talk to her directly. Regardless (and it should go without saying), the lady will have a say in the matter.

It should not be surprising that your feelings toward this lady are mutual and that she is honored by your desire to get to know her more intimately. If this be the case, then we are excited for you. But what does this step mean, and how should you go about the relationship from here?

The Relationship from This Point On

Perhaps the best way of progressing further is for you and the lady to identify some core convictions and guidelines. In doing so, we encourage you to keep them simple and reasonable, but above all they should be founded in wisdom.

We really want to stress the importance of creating for yourselves guidelines that are simple and reasonable. The Lord's ways are not meant to be burdensome, and so there is no need to create unnecessary perimeters that will only strain your relationship.

You may want to ask yourselves various questions and create your guidelines accordingly. For example, will you both agree to work out any differences that arise in your relationship, rather than quickly conclude that you are not meant for one another? Do you both agree to refrain completely from physical intimacy as the Scriptures promote until that day you are finally wed (1 Cor. 7:1-2)? These and other important questions should be considered before your relationship progresses.

The Proposal

At some point, you will both likely experience some sort of mutual confirmation that you want to marry one another. There is no way for us to tell you how you will come to know this, for the ways of love and commitment are the subject of countless songs, ballads, novels, and dramas, each describing a unique manner in which boy meets girl. But when you do know, we ask that you make certain to write and tell us the story of how you and your bride came to be.

And while we are being bold with our requests, might we ask that you send a couple of wedding invitations if you do take our previous advice about that pig roast? We would be honored to attend...!

Made for Fatherhood

During our last lesson, called "Made for Marriage," we discussed how the institution of marriage first came to be, and we identified several important qualities of a godly marriage, all with the intent to solidify a foundation regarding this important topic. In doing so, we placed a special emphasis on the relationship that you will one day have with your bride-to-be. But your marriage will not affect just the relationship you have with your bride. In fact, the union of your spirits will possibly be the *very cause* of additional relationships, for together you will quite likely bring forth into this world children of your own!

We can already imagine some of the different reactions that you might have upon initially reading this lesson. Perhaps you have instantly broken into a cold sweat, for you fear you are not even ready to do tomorrow's chores, let alone raise a family. Or maybe you consider the matter unimportant, for you figure that fatherhood is something that probably won't happen until you're really old. Or perhaps you are properly sober about the whole matter, knowing that in due time the privilege of being a father will present itself, but in the meantime you still have your go-cart to fix.

Whether you have never given the matter any thought, or if you have been wanting children all your life, your reactions are probably within the realm of normalcy. But as with any important topic of life, we want you to be *complete in Christ*, and that involves having a godly understanding of what God thinks about things. And most assuredly, God is not silent about the topic of fatherhood.

God Ordained

Like the institution of marriage, parenthood is ordained by God. Make no mistake about it—God created the earth with the intention that it be filled with people. The Genesis narrative makes this clear:

> *And God created man in His own image, in the image of God He created him; male and female He created them. And God blessed them; and God said to them, "Be fruitful and multiply, and fill the earth, and subdue it; and rule over...every living thing that moves on the earth."*   *Genesis 1:27-28*

"Be fruitful and multiply," God has said. And His word is still the same today. There is nothing to indicate that God's views on this matter have changed. He has a vested interest in people. He loves and places tremendous value on them, so much so that He has made provision for their every need.

You should know that there are plenty of people who are clueless about the ordination of parenthood. And there are others, who, knowing better, simply disregard God's say on the matter. As you might suspect, such people have embraced a faulty worldview, and thus are blind to the truth. One false view in this regard is not at all uncommon, and you should know something about it:

The Earth as Mother

It is likely you have heard the phrase "Mother Nature" many

times. While there is nothing inherently wrong with this phrase, you should know that many people take the wording quite literally. They believe that the earth originally brought forth all of the life on it, and hence the phrase and others like it. This worldview is not a new one, and has likely been around for thousands of years. But it is a ridiculous and ungodly worldview.

Science itself recognizes that life must come from life, but many scientists make an exception to this law when it comes to the origin of living things. In doing so, they conveniently disregard common sense, and ultimately, God. They believe that long ago, lifeless molecules, coupled with energy and lots of time, spontaneously gave birth to crude, microscopic forms of life that eventually evolved into everything else that is living. They believe that the earth is their parent, rather than acknowledging God as their creator.

At the heart of this worldview is the notion that mankind is here because of the earth, rather than the earth being here for the benefit of mankind. However, God commissioned mankind to "be fruitful and multiply" and to "fill the earth and subdue it." But this false worldview does not see things this way, and in fact often makes mankind out to be the enemy of the earth. Proponents of this worldview often argue that mankind has filled the earth and subdued it so much so that he has now overpopulated and begun to destroy it.

Plenty of Room

The notion that mankind has overpopulated the earth is a myth, and it has neither a scientific nor sensible basis. The people who believe this false view have probably never travelled more than three city blocks, or they are just plain blind to the vastness of the earth. Indeed, the earth is vast, and you can be sure that if God made it to be the home of His children, He would also make provision in regard to room.

Here's an interesting fact to help clarify this point: Did you know that you could line up all the people in the entire world side-by-side, chest-to-back, and fit them *all* within the city limits of Jacksonville, Florida? In fact, there would be plenty of wiggle room, and much of the city would still be vacant! Feel free to do a little fact-finding and make the calculations yourself if you should need convincing.

Of course, it would not be any fun to live in such a small space all the time. After an hour or so, everybody would want to go home and take a good shower. However, a point can be made, and that is there is *lots* of room on this wonderful planet of ours. And you can be sure that God designed the earth to be able to sustain us with plenty of food and other resources. In fact, the state of Iowa alone can produce enough food to feed the entire world (although you may tire of corn and soybeans three times a day). When you hear that certain areas of the world do not have enough resources, poor economic conditions due to inefficient governments are often to blame.

As Christians, we must never forget that God loves people. And because He loves mankind, you can be sure that He made the earth with ample room and other provisions to take care of all our needs.

A Blessing from the Lord

We lament that there are certain people who do not place a high value on humanity. "There are already enough people in the world; we do not need any more," they say. Others, recognizing this view to be extreme, temper their attitudes somewhat by saying, "It's hard to provide for so many children, so it's best not to have very many."

But what does God's Word say? Without exception, every biblical passage involving children refers to them as intended blessings! Consider this verse: "Then the Lord your God will prosper you abundantly in all the work of your hand, in the offspring of your body. He will also bless the fruit of your womb" (Deut. 30:9). Or how about this one?: "Like arrows in the hand of a warrior, so are the children of one's youth. How blessed is the man whose quiver is full of them!" (Psalm 127:4-5).

Here's yet another verse (one of our favorites), which comes right from the mouth of Jesus: "Permit the children to come to Me; do not hinder them; for the kingdom of God belongs to such as these" (Mark 10:14).

Children are indeed an intended blessing! And yet, there are those that do not recognize this wonderful truth. Some, while recognizing part of the truth, attempt to keep God's blessings at bay by suggesting that less is better than more. One wise man offered a thought provoking question in this regard. He asked, "If children are a blessing from the Lord, why do some couples tell the Lord that they want a limit on their blessing?"

One day, you may have children of your own. And when you do, we hope you keep them coming! Embrace the idea of having as many children as the Lord will provide, so that "your quiver will be full."

What About Provision?

We have already assured you that there is plenty of room and food in the world. But make no mistake about it, a house will not be made for you, nor will food magically appear on your plate without you having to work for it. It is likely that you are already keenly aware of this fact, both from your own experiences as well as the lessons you have previously learned in Teleo Scouts.

Some couples are reluctant to want children because they are fearful of either their own abilities to provide or of God's ability to do His part. So we will offer here a word of encouragement on this matter. But we will not be flowery or long-winded in doing so.

Simply stated, you have nothing to worry about in regard to providing for your family some day. In fact, you won't even need an extra edge; all you will need to see your family through is a solid work ethic and an ability to see needs and fulfill them Can you do this? Of course you can! We have no doubt about it, and neither should you.

But what about God's ability to do His part? In short, God can be trusted to take care of you and your future family, every time, all the time. We have never met one individual who could honestly tell us otherwise after placing his trust in God. God would not indicate that children are a blessing from Him, and then not provide appropriate shelter, clothing, and food for them. The idea is just silly. If God blesses you with one child, He will provide accordingly. And if He blesses you with two, three, ten or even thirty children, He will still provide accordingly!

Even a young girl will feed and care for her Shirley Temple doll. Why, we have even seen some boys feed their GI Joes pretend K-rations. If it is human nature to provide for those under our care, how much more will our perfect, heavenly Father take care of us!

You will do well to always remember that part of the Sermon on the Mount which we studied earlier. Jesus told us not to worry about what we will eat or what we will wear, for if we seek first after the kingdom, then "…all these things will be added to you" (Matt. 6:33).

You are quite likely going to be a dad someday. We encourage you to not let the concern of provision be a stumbling block to you. It is a non-issue. God is looking forward to working alongside you, helping to lead your family. Remember too, that your children are His children; He will not let them go without provision any more than He would let you go without.

When Should You Have Children?

There are some married couples who try hard to plan when they will have children and how many they will finally settle on. While we are not going to dissuade you from one day giving these matters thought, neither will we emphasize their importance.

If you keep on the forefront of your mind that children are an intended blessing from the Lord and that God is a wonderful provider, then ninety percent or more of your concerns about family planning will be instantly taken care of.

So, should you have children soon after you are married, or should you wait? Our counsel to you is to let God be truly in control in all matters related to this issue. Neither attempt to accelerate nor slow the matter, and let the wonder of it all unfold naturally.

How to Keep a Blessing a Blessing

We have unabashedly declared what the Bible says about children—that they are an intended blessing from the Lord. That being said, we know that some people doubt that children are a blessing because they have seen so much selfishness and other bad manners coming from various children. So is the Bible true? How can we honestly state that children are a blessing when so many of them demonstrate otherwise?

The Bible says that children are *meant* to be blessings; but it does not imply that all children are, in fact, blessings as far as their behaviors are concerned. Cain was most assuredly not a blessing when he killed his brother Abel. The great judge Samuel could not keep his son in line. And King David's son Absalom certainly gave him grief.

Why do some children turn out to be the opposite of a blessing? As we have stated in a previous lesson, God has gifted each person with a free will, which means that all of us are ultimately responsible for the decisions that we make in life. The power and responsibility associated with a free will cannot be overstated. Nobody forced Cain to kill Abel, and likewise nobody is forced to choose evil over good. But it is clear that many children grow up and choose to live dishonorable lives. The Bible is rich in content about this very topic, and it offers valuable insight in regard to raising children so that they will not choose to live the wrong way. Let's review some of what the Bible has to say:

A Wonderful Proverb—To Train Up a Child

One of the most oft quoted verses pertaining to raising children is Proverbs 22:16, which states, "Train up a child in the way he should go; even when he is old he will not depart from it."

Notice that the first word in this passage says "train." It does not say "provide for," "teach," or even "raise." It says, pointedly enough, that your children will need to be *trained*. Too many parents miss this foundational point. Indeed, the world is full of parents who think that clothing their children and sending them off to bed is enough. It is not enough!

If you want your dog to come, sit, roll over, or do any kind of trick or obey any kind of command, you must train it. Rover is simply not going to fetch or do anything other than eat, sleep, or scratch himself unless he is trained by someone to do otherwise. If this is true for a lowly dog, how much more so is it for humans who are infinitely more complex!

You should know that there is a popular worldview that competes with the biblical one we are presenting here. This false worldview says that because humans are complex and have a free will, they should not be trained. Rather, they should be free to do whatever they want, even throughout childhood. If Little Johnny wants scrambled eggs for breakfast after he requested Cheerios and was granted them, then Mommy or Daddy should instantly comply. If Sister Susie wants her eyebrow pierced for her first day of kindergarten, then her wish should be granted. In some places, this false worldview has been embraced so much that it has become the cultural norm. As you might suspect, this approach to childrearing tends to raise children who have respect neither for God, themselves, nor for others.

In The Way He Should Go

The proverb tells us to train a child "in the way he should go." Some parents find this part of the passage mysterious and even intimidating, for they aren't sure what the phrase means. But really this part of the verse is not mysterious at all.

"In the way he should go" does not refer to a north or south type of direction. Neither does it refer to guiding a child toward a particular vocation in life. While it may involve some of these aspects, the verse primarily intends to admonish its readers to lead their children in the *path of righteousness.*

Jesus told us that the road to heaven is a narrow one, and that few find its path (Matt. 7:14). One day, when you are a father, you will need to identify this path for your children, and after identifying it, you will need to use wisdom to train them how to walk accordingly.

When He Is Old....

If you train your sons and daughters to walk in the way of righteousness, they will have a huge advantage all throughout their lives, and this includes their old age. So then, we will offer, in the way of tips and commentary, some insight from the Bible and from experiences gathered from those who have walked successfully before us.

Some Tips for Success:

Before we begin offering you a few tips in the way of parenting, you should know that space and time do not permit us to present all you will need to know. So we will not be discussing the finer points of changing diapers or the drawbacks of bottled formula in this lesson. You and your wife will figure these things out and more in due time. Actually, most parenting skills aren't all that hard to master, and we are confident that you and your wife will both be experts sooner than you think.

However, there are certain things we deem important enough to pass on. Most of what you are about to read is wisdom passed on from ages past; we have invented nothing. Some of it is universally accepted, and other parts are downright resisted due to conflicting worldviews. But all of it is presented so that you can keep the hearts of your children in the path of righteousness.

Dad and Mom in Agreement

Before you and your bride-to-be have children, you must both understand and mutually embrace the importance of being in agreement as to how you will raise them. Indeed, the more you can agree on this matter, the better. In fact, total agreement is best. The power of unity in this regard cannot be overemphasized. Parental harmony fosters emotional security, safeguards against domestic divisiveness, and validates all things taught.

The Dad as Leader

How do you promote an environment of unity between you and your wife with respect to childrearing? The best way is to choose a wife who embraces all the Bible has to say about this subject, and one who will let you lead in this regard. We already discussed the importance of this in our last lesson, "Made for Marriage," but it is worth repeating here.

How your children will be schooled, how they will be disciplined, and who they will hang out with are just a few of the many questions you and your wife will need to answer. But make no mistake about it; you will need to be in charge. Ephesians 5:23 says, "For the husband is the head of the wife, as Christ also is the head of the church, He Himself being the Savior of the body."

You may have seen some families whereby neither the father nor the mother was in charge. Rather, it was the children who were directing the course of daily living. May this never be in your home! Children should never be allowed to tell Dad or Mom what is right for the moment. You must make sure your children are not raised to do so.

We are not saying that it is wrong to ask your toddler if he wants ice cream along with his birthday cake; you may in fact want to ask him questions like this from time to time. But he should never *tell* you what he wants. Before long, he will be telling you he wants the car keys, and he may even chide you for not filling the gas tank.

Teach Them Your Way

Asking children questions in the way of preferences should not be the norm, especially if the children are very young. Parents who routinely ask their toddlers what they would like to wear or what they prefer for lunch are only asking for problems down the road. If you adopt this type of parenting style, you will likely raise a child to be self-centered. You shouldn't be surprised if you are routinely challenged by such a child.

Perhaps a short example can be useful here. We know of

one family who went on a vacation in a beautiful, mountainous region of our country. There were a few historical sites along the way that both the father and mother really wanted to see, but in the end they never ended up visiting them. The reason? The parents made the mistake of asking their young children if they wanted to visit the sites. Both the young son and his slightly older sister instantly voiced objections to their parents. "We don't want to do what you guys want. We would rather have extra time for swimming and watching television at a hotel."

The father complied with his children's wishes rather than his own or his wife's, and both parents felt like they were being sacrificial servants to their children. But the truth of the matter is these children were already in a routine of being moody and steering their parents accordingly, and both Mom and Dad were blind to it.

These children and their parents missed out on some really terrific experiences that they may never be able to recapture. Could these parents have directed their family in a better way? We think so, and that is by not letting their children dictate family policy.

Truth be told, children do not have a clue what they really want, let alone what is best for them. It is usually not until they are in their early teens that they are able to reasonably analyze what they want based on prior experiences. Even then, they are often governed by the extremes of what-is-familiar and what-is-new. While this is normal for most people, children are not usually equipped to make wise decisions in this regard, especially when consideration is made for the good of the entire family.

When your children get older, it will be natural for them to voice their requests and offer insight into family affairs, and it should be just as natural for you to want to hear and consider them. A request from your twelve year old son to visit a sporting goods store so he can check out a new fishing lure that he has saved up for is a reasonable request that you may want to consider. However, a request from a six year old to stop at McDonald's for his fifth Happy Meal in the same week is probably more noise than anything else. In many successful families, such requests are not even allowed.

There is a philosophy on the loose that suggests that parents are somehow being mean if they direct their children confidently and with consistent certainty. This philosophy is wishy-washy, and you will do well to reject it before you even have children. If you and your wife want to see Custer's Last Stand during a family vacation and you think your children would benefit from it, then your way should be the sole voice of direction. Your word should not be the last word; it should be the first and only word. This should hold true for all matters regarding childrearing.

Godly Expression

Do you want to be the kind of father someday that is a really good leader, the kind where his words are like golden music whether they be in the form of a directive or an announcement of things to come? If so, then you will do well to incorporate a healthy and bountiful dose of godly expression in both your *demeanor* and *candor*.

Your demeanor is the way in which you behave and conduct yourself. Essentially, it is the expression of your personality. Your candor is part of your demeanor because it demonstrates the sincerity of your expression. In other words, a person's candor indicates whether or not he is genuine. In regard to both of these expressions, your desire should be that your children may see God through you. As God is certain, so should you be. As God is love, so should you be. And as God is gracious, so should you be.

In an upcoming lesson, we will be discussing the various fruit of the Holy Spirit, which is comprised of love, joy, peace, longsuffering, kindness, goodness, faithfulness, gentleness, and self-control (Gal. 5:22). You will be a godly father indeed if your demeanor and candor reflect these wonderful things.

Being Joyful

We view joy as one of the most effective expressions in raising godly children. We have already indicated that as a father, you must be in charge, and that your word should be the first and only. If we had said only that, one might likely conclude that childrearing was a lifeless contest of the wills. But as we have stated, children are an intended blessing, and you will certainly find joy upon joy while raising your children.

If you want to stack the deck in your favor in regard to gaining honor and respect from your children, then you will do well to let your children *know* that they bring you joy. You can do this in many ways, not the least of which is to simply smile at them. And let your smiles turn to laughter from time to time, even often.

Do you know how to tickle your son or daughter's funny bone? Then do so, both literally and figuratively. Tell them jokes, be at ease with them, and allow yourself to be the brunt of humor from time to time.

Have you seen your son make a fantastic tackle or your daughter make a graceful expression? Then tell them so in a way that clearly demonstrates the joy within you.

Can a parent do all of this too much? Actually, we think so. You do not want to be the type of father that is clowning around so much so that he is difficult to take seriously. In fact, your children should not ever have to search for the serious side of you, so don't mask it by giving them the idea that fun and laughter is your number one aim. That being said, be lavish with your praise and admiration of your children's accomplishments.

Spending Time

We will not offer advice in the way of exactly how much time you should spend with your children. Suffice it to say that the gray-haired veterans who have parented before us are right; time goes by very quickly, and before one realizes it, his children are grown. So you will want to keep this in mind, and make the most of your time with your children while you have it.

That being said, we should let you know that some parents get into a trap whereby the entire routine of the family revolves around keeping the schedule of their children's various commitments. We encourage you to guard against having everything centered around your children such that you are always taking them to or from some sort of practice or event. To be sure, there will be times when this is best for them, but do not think this needs to be a lifelong habit.

While we are on this topic, we want to encourage you to spend plenty of time alone with your wife after you have children. And don't be afraid of going overboard on this matter. Your children will need to see that their mother comes before them, and it will do them good if they are told this directly and for them to see this in practice.

How we wish that we did not have to warn you against the sin of becoming obsessed with work, but alas! Many men have fallen prey to the slave-master of labor. While we encourage you to be a hard and steady worker, we will also warn you against doing so to the detriment of your family. We would rather see you serve bread without butter and have time for your family than to see you serve steak and shrimp without having time for them.

Start Them Young

When should you formally start childrearing? We say right

away! A practice that we have seen employed successfully many times is to give a newborn immediate and consistent attention for each and every need during the first several months of his life. Coddle him, pamper him, and feed him until he is satisfied once again. By doing so, you will be well on your way to raising a child who knows for certain that his world is a safe one.

When They Start to Test You

Up to about seven months of age, give or take, the only noises a baby knows how to make are soft cooing sounds along with intermittent crying. One thing you must know is that babies do not whine at this age, for all they know how to do is cry. Crying is completely natural, for it is a baby's God-given way of letting his parent know that something is wrong. However, whining is another matter.

Whining begins when a baby starts to be more cognitive of his world. This usually happens at about seven months of age, and during this time an observant parent will notice that his or her baby will sometimes "cry" for no legitimate reason. It is at this time that a baby will experiment with whining.

An unobservant parent will mistake whining for crying and will inadvertently encourage the baby to whine even more by giving him attention. We implore you to heed this advice: do not ever pamper a whining baby! This is a pivotal time in the development of your child and much is at stake, not the least of which is your future ability to see your child as a consistent blessing. Simply stated, you must have the courage and insight to discern the difference between a cry and a whine, and then to respond appropriately.

Why do we say it takes "courage" to discern a cry from a whine? We say "courage" because too many parents are fearful of facing the truth that left to their own devices and without godly direction, babies will eventually grow into self-centered toddlers who will eventually grow into misdirected children who will eventually grow into egocentric teenagers who will...you get the picture.

All humans, at one point or another in their lives, will try to test their boundaries to see what is acceptable and safe and what is not. It should not surprise anyone, then, that this testing begins at a very early age, earlier than most parents are willing to realize.

This testing begins by whining. For example, a baby will sometimes whine, rather than cry, because it wants to be picked up after being put to bed. Pick the baby up after whining, and what have you done? You have just taught him that it is all right to whine to get picked up. After a few more times of this, it becomes clear who trained whom. The baby will have successfully trained the parent to succumb to his manipulative whining.

So what is a parent to do? We encourage all parents of newborns to calmly and confidently declare war on forms of whining in their household. And to be sure—whining takes many forms. Sometimes it will be more of a squawk than a whine; other times it may be more like a screech. The older a baby gets, the more varied the forms. Perhaps you have heard some of the various forms of whining coming from a teenager. If so, you know how utterly awful it can sound by this advanced stage. But chances are good that a whining teenager was once a whining baby who was never successfully restrained.

Parents do not need to get upset when whining happens; rather, they simply need to respond consistently in love. A baby who whines should be completely ignored if at all possible. If eye contact must be made, the parent should convey a look of disapproval. A firm yet confident "no" should somehow also be conveyed. Babies that are still whining after being placed in bed should be gently but firmly held in the prone position and not allowed to move. A gentle lullaby might be sung by the parent, not as a reward for whining but rather as a supplement to being firmly held. In a very short time the baby will be having heavenly dreams of your lullabies.

A very young baby who is whining during waking hours should be held gently yet firmly against his parent's chest, and not allowed to squirm, not even a little. A gentle but confident "no" should be whispered into the baby's ear. If the squirming or whining increases, the firm hold upon baby should actually increase. At all costs, you must win. Do not give into the baby's demand.

In short order, any baby, even strong-willed ones, will tire and comply. After all, they want to know their boundaries, and once they are convinced that you are in complete control, they will not want to waste energy on a battle that they know that they will only lose.

Why are we spending so much time discussing something as seemingly trivial as whining? Isn't a lesson on how to stop thumb sucking more important? No, it is not. Whining is the precursor to murmuring and complaining, two of the most destructive attitudes that a person could demonstrate. You will do well to eliminate it in your children at a very young age. Once you do, the rest becomes easier, and you will see them as constant blessings.

Arguing

Can you imagine somebody attempting to argue with God? The idea is as much grotesque as it is silly. It is dishonoring, to say the least, and a complete exercise in futility. It is also grotesque and silly to see a child attempt an argument with his or her parents, and you will do well to not let your children even attempt such folly.

Arguing is actually an evil cousin to whining. There are all kinds of ways to prevent it from taking root, but space does not permit us to discuss them here. Suffice it to say that wisdom and discretion will see you through. There are also some decent books on the matter for the looking, and there are plenty of parents who will gladly share with you their tricks for success. At any rate, we thought we should mention this topic in case you think that arguing with parents is normal. It's not. But we will at least leave you with a word of encouragement: if you can manage to take care of whining during the infant years, you more than likely will not ever have to deal with its evil cousin.

Discipline

Discipline is any training that corrects, molds, or perfects one's moral character. The Bible has much to say regarding discipline, including the fact that God disciplines his own children:

> *It is for discipline that you endure; God deals with you as with sons; for what son is there whom his father does not discipline? But if you are without discipline, of which all have become partakers, then you are illegitimate children and not sons. Furthermore, we had earthly fathers to discipline us, and we respected them; shall we not much rather be subject to the Father of spirits, and live? For they disciplined us for a short time as seemed best to them, but He disciplines us for our good, so that we may share His holiness. All discipline for the moment seems not to be joyful, but sorrowful; yet to those who have been trained by it, afterwards it yields the peaceful fruit of righteousness.* Heb. 12:7-11

Discipline is indeed a good thing. Proverbs 12:1 tells us, "Whoever loves discipline loves knowledge, but he who hates reproof is stupid." So how are children best disciplined? There are several ways to do so, and you will need to study this matter out as part of good fathering.

In our culture, "time outs" and "responsible thinking times" have taken the place of customary corporal chastisement (spankings), which were at one time embraced by most of our culture. Most kinds of discipline techniques can find some sort of biblical justification, but we will caution you to refrain from the cultural tendency to refrain from spanking. The Bible has much to say about this.

Consider these biblical verses on the subject of chastisement: "He who withholds his rod hates his son, but he who loves him disciplines him diligently" (Prov. 13:24); "Foolishness is bound up in the heart of a child; the rod of discipline will remove it far from him" (Prov. 22:15); and "The rod and reproof give wisdom, but a child who gets his own way brings shame to his mother" (Prov. 29:15).

While these proverbs demonstrate the importance and usefulness of corporal punishment, they also indicate several realities that go against cultural acceptance. We see that spanking is an act of love, but refraining from spanking is not (13:24). We see that it is normal for a child to sometimes act foolishly and that it is a good thing to remove foolishness from him (22:15). And we see that a selfish child is an embarrassment to his parent, but correction can produce wisdom (29:15). When you are a father some day, hold these principles dear to you, and you will have a solid foundation on which to build.

Wisdom and Discretion

You will not be able to be an effective father if you do not employ wisdom. What exactly is wisdom? Wisdom has many facets, not the least of which are common sense and sound judgment. How does one obtain wisdom? Thank the Lord that obtaining wisdom is relatively easy! Proverbs 20:21-22 says, "Wisdom shouts in the street, she lifts her voice in the square;

at the head of the noisy streets she cries out; at the entrance of the gates in the city she utters her sayings...." And James 1:5 says, "But if any of you lacks wisdom, let him ask of God, who gives to all generously and without reproach, and it will be given to him."

So we can see that wisdom is not something that is hard to find, nor something revealed to us in mysterious whispers. Wisdom wants to be heard and in fact will "shout loudly" to anyone who has ears to hear.

But common sense and sound judgment are not enough. These will provide the insight that you need for a given matter, but you will need *prudence* and *discretion* as well. Prudence is the ability to anticipate the probable results of one's actions. And you will need to top this off with *discretion*, which is the ability to properly respond to your judgment of a matter. This might sound complicated, but really it isn't. Much of it involves studying human behavior, and so you will need to be a student of your own children. In a short time, you will be able to discern the motivation of almost anything that they do, and you will be able to predict with fair certainty the best way to respond to them. Thank God for wisdom!

Being a Role Model

This section of our lesson should stand apart as being the most important. As a man, you are to be God's light to the world. As a husband, you are to demonstrate the sacrificial love of Jesus. And as a father, you are to be all these things and more, for you are to demonstrate the very nature of God. In doing so, you will point to Jesus, for He is the perfect way. But make no mistake about it; your children's ability to understand God as their Father is largely dependent on your ability to make Him known to them.

As a father to your children, you must be willing and able to say to them, as Paul said to the church at Corinth, "Be imitators of me, just as I also am of Christ" (1 Cor. 11:1). We trust that you will be willing and able to do so, for your children will need to hear this challenge and for you to show them the way.

In the meantime, identify for yourself the positive role models in your own life. Consider your own father, your friends' fathers, or other men whom you may know. Do you see leadership skills within certain men that make you proud and hopeful that you can be like them someday? If so, good! Not one of these men would fault you for copying them. On the contrary, they would be honored.

Teach Them Diligently

Here is an oft quoted passage in regard to childrearing. No study on this subject would be complete without it:

> *Hear, O Israel! The Lord is our God, the Lord is one! You shall love the Lord your God with all your heart and with all your soul and with all your might. These words, which I am commanding you today, shall be on your heart. You shall teach them diligently to your sons and shall talk of them when you sit in your house and when you walk by the way and when you lie down and when you rise up. You shall bind them as a sign on your hand and they shall be as frontals on your forehead. You shall write them on the doorposts of your house and on your gates.* *Deuteronomy 6:5-9*

We view this passage as one of the most informative and liberating ones in all of Scripture regarding childrearing. It tells us, simply, to have God's words "on our heart" and to teach His words to our children at all times. Does this mean that you are supposed to lead your family in a round-the-clock family devotion? Heavens, no! It means that you are to teach your children the precepts of God as a natural expression of who you are.

From time to time, even often, take opportunities to make important points come alive to your children. Do so at all kinds of various times, whether you are working, playing, dining, or traveling together. While study guides and Sunday morning sermons are useful tools for teaching children, there really is no substitute for hearing their father's unique take on a matter.

At the heart of this matter is your children's education. We implore you to seek and obtain the very best education that you possibly can for them. If homeschooling is the best option, then by all means do so! If certain people are better able to teach specific subject matters, then solicit and obtain their expertise. But in doing so, never compromise on what you know to be best for your children. This is true for many facets of their upbringing, but especially so in regard to education.

You—A Future Dad!

So, what do you think of all this? Can you see yourself as a father some day? If you are a committed follower of Jesus Christ, then we can see you as one, and a great one at that.

Someday, you will likely be the proud father of someone who looks and maybe even acts quite a bit like you. He or she will be made in your image, and it is just fine for you to allow yourself to imagine what this time will be like. We hope you look forward to it, for the world needs more people like you.

We realize that this lesson is a bit different than most of the others. For one, you are not called or even ready to implement the knowledge you have learned at this time. Nevertheless, you are getting old enough and wise enough to know that time passes quickly by. In due time, fatherhood will be upon you. In the meantime, we realize you may have more pressing needs, like fixing your go-cart. But you will do us proud if every once in a while between now and then, that you think of these things with wonderful anticipation!

The Fruit of the Holy Spirit

If you have been a keen reader of your Teleo Scouts lessons, you will have noticed that we have referred to the *fruit of the Holy Spirit* from time to time. We did so in "Treating Ladies Properly" when pointing out that true beauty involves bearing the Spirit's fruit. We discussed peace as part of the Spirit's fruit in "A Lesson on Peace." In our study entitled "Being a Good Steward," we expressed the importance of responsibly bearing fruit. And in "Made for Fatherhood," we discussed how vital it is for a father to demonstrate good fruit if he hopes to raise his children well. In each of these lessons, we indicated that we would discuss the fruit of the Holy Spirit in greater depth in a future lesson. We are now delivering on our word....

What is "The Fruit"?

As you may recall, the term "fruit of the Holy Spirit" comes from a passage in Paul's letter to the Galatians. Commonly, the passage is quoted in part as such: "...the fruit of the Spirit is love, joy, peace, patience, kindness, goodness, faithfulness, gentleness, self-control..." (5:22).

If you are the kind of fellow who gets easily befuddled when common language is used figuratively, you may be wondering why words like "love" and "joy" are described as fruit. After all, love and joy are not usually for sale in the fruit and produce section of your grocery store. And you may have picked apples or cherries directly from a tree, but you haven't likely heard of a peace or patience tree.

However, the fruit of the Spirit is not something that you can literally taste, see, or otherwise perceive with your senses. Rather, it is comprised of various virtues. A virtue, as you may recall, is an admirable trait associated with one's character. And like apples or oranges, the Spirit's fruit grows, beginning with something relatively small which blooms and ending with something beautiful and ripe to be used by others.

Did you know that the various types of fruit that can be literally eaten, like grapes or strawberries, first had their beginnings as flowers? And the flowers, in order to thrive, first had to be part of a branch. Of course, the various branches of the plant had to first grow from a central branch. This is true for all kinds of fruit-bearing plants. Well, the same is true for *spiritual fruit*.

Jesus explained all of this in an easy-to-understand passage in the gospel of John. In doing so, He referred to a type of fruit that grows on vines. Most likely He referred to grapes, which can be eaten whole, made into jellies, or pressed to make juice or fine wines. The passage says,

"I am the true vine, and My Father is the vinedresser. Every branch in Me that does not bear fruit, He takes away; and every branch that bears fruit, He prunes it so that it may bear more fruit.... "As the branch cannot bear fruit of itself unless it abides in the vine, so neither can you unless you abide in Me. I am the vine, you are the branches; he who abides in Me and I in him, he bears much fruit, for apart from Me you can do nothing. If anyone does not abide in Me, he is thrown away as a branch and dries up; and they gather them, and cast them into the fire and they are burned.... "My Father is glorified by this, that you bear much fruit, and so prove

to be My disciples."   *John 15:1, 2, 4-8*

So you can see that the fruit we are talking about in this lesson is spiritual fruit. It manifests itself in the form of various virtues, like love, joy, peace, patience, kindness, goodness, faithfulness, gentleness, and self-control.

We will refer back to this particular passage a little later in our lesson, but first we need to clarify an important detail....

Fruit or Fruits?

If you are the kind of fellow who naturally counts things, you may have noticed that there are nine types of fruit listed in Galatians 5:22. Does this mean that there are only nine kinds of fruit that come from the Spirit? What about wit, humor, contentment, discretion, bravery, and the host of other virtues that, by all accounts, come from God? Are these not also kinds of fruits that the Spirit bears? You bet they are!

So why, then, are there only nine listed? Are the nine listed the most important ones? What about the others? Actually, this line of questioning might cause us to end up missing the whole point of the matter. Truth be told, the writer of Galatians describes the fruit of the Holy Spirit as being *singular*. Read it again if you missed this important detail in your first analysis: "...the *fruit* of the Spirit is love, joy, peace, patience, kindness, goodness, faithfulness, gentleness, self-control..."

So then, there is one kind of fruit that the Spirit produces, and that is the cumulation of the various virtues that are manifested in a Christian's personality. Does this seem abstract? If so, think of several different kinds of literal fruits, perfectly blended together so that a singular fruit is produced, such that this singular fruit is yummier and more satisfying than any one of the fruits from which it was comprised. This is the Spirit's wonderful way—He is able to take all of your virtues and produce from it your personality, which is the glorious expression of who you are!

A Primer on the Spirit

It's quite likely that you already have a pretty good handle on who the Holy Spirit is and what He is all about. But just to be sure, it's probably a good idea to provide a short primer:

Suffice it to say, the Spirit is far more important than the fruit that He bears. After all, "Apart from Me you can do nothing."

The Spirit is the very essence of God and of His Son, Jesus. He is the "Spirit of Life" (Rom. 8:2) and the one who "gives life" (2 Cor. 3:2). He is "holy" as only God is holy (Eph. 1:13, Isaiah 57:15). The Holy Spirit can speak (Acts 28:25-27), and be grieved and lied to (Eph. 4:30, Acts 5:3-4). Moreover, He literally *lives in* those who believe in Jesus' holy name (1 Cor. 3:16; Eph. 2:21,22).

So you can see that the Holy Spirit is not merely some kind of impersonal, "active force" as the foolish cult members who go door-to-door might claim. On the contrary, the Spirit is very personal, for He has the very personality of God.

It should not surprise you, then, that the Holy Spirit has a *divine role* in all Christians' lives. Before Jesus died, He told His disciples that it was actually to their benefit that He would be leaving them, for in doing so He would also send to them the Holy Spirit:

> *"But I tell you the truth, it is to your advantage that I go away; for if I do not go away, the Helper will not come to you; but if I go, I will send Him to you. And He, when He comes, will convict the world concerning sin and righteousness and judgment; concerning sin, because they do not believe in Me; and concerning righteousness,*

because I go to the Father and you no longer see Me; and concerning judgment, because the ruler of this world has been judged....But when He, the Spirit of truth, comes, He will guide you into all the truth...." John 16:7-9, 13

After Jesus died, was resurrected, and ascended into heaven, He sent the "Helper" as He promised, and the church was in fact baptized into the Holy Spirit (Acts 1:4-8, 2:1-4). Prior to this time, only kings and priests were able to go into the tabernacle to encounter God, but now God's Holy Spirit resides with power in anyone for the simple asking and receiving of the same by faith!

There is much more that can be taught about the person of the Holy Spirit, and in fact entire books are written on the matter. Some of these books are terrific at enlightening the truth of the gospel. Others are not fit for the fire, for the devil's grease does not burn well. But if you can embrace what we have presented here, you will be nine tenths or more of the way to a mature understanding of the Holy Spirit.

Virtue Described

As we observed, there are nine manifestations of the Spirit's fruit listed in the passage of Galatians that we initially read. And as we discussed, these are only some of the many which are grown by the Spirit. In truth, there are scores of them. That being said, it is useful to discuss the ones that are cited in the passage. We will list them again here, just for good measure: "...the fruit of the Spirit is love, joy, peace, patience, kindness, goodness, faithfulness, gentleness, self-control..."

Love

We suppose that most of our readers are the quick witted types who catch on fairly easily. After all, such is the hope of a Teleo Scout and for that matter, all mature Christians. However, we realize that not everyone fits this description, and so we offer clarification for the dull of mind:

When we talk about love in terms of the Spirit's fruit, we are not talking about the love that one may have for *things*. The Spirit does not bless a Christian with a supernatural ability to love his baseball card collection, his canoe, or even his paintball gun. No man needs the Spirit's help to love such things. In fact, without the presence of the Holy Spirit, a man is actually more likely to magnify his love for things. Egad that one should ever need to receive this correction!

On the contrary, the Spirit blesses a Christian with a measure of love *for people*. This measure of love, voluntarily submitted to God for nurturing and cultivation, grows into virtue. Virtue then becomes a nourishing fruit that God can use to bring liberation and joy into the lives of others. Make love for people your life's aim, and you will be a blessed man indeed.

If you are the type of boy who loves ice cream cones more than he does his own siblings, or the kind of boy who prefers the company of plastic army men over his parents or friends, then we fear for you. But we will not dwell too much on presenting a rebuke here. Most likely this does not describe you, and so we will move on…

Suffice it to say, love is the royal expression of all virtues. We stated previously that the fruit of the Holy Spirit is kind of like blending several different kinds of literal fruits together to produce a singular fruit which is superior in the sum of its parts. Well, love is the quintessential fruit in such a blend. Without love, the rest of the concoction would instantly spoil.

You may think we are overstating the importance of love when we say that the fruit of the Holy Spirit would go bad without it. But we are not overstating the matter. In fact, without love, everything spoils in such a way that it fumigates its immediate area with a toxic gas fit only for the devil to breathe.

The toxic gas produced in the absence of love is odorless and colorless to most people; it takes a discerning nose and eye to sense it for what it really is. Normally, this gas does not kill instantly. Rather, it puts its victims into a subtle state of stupor whereby they are numb to the reality of their condition. At best, a victim may survive but will never thrive. At worst, he will be so full of himself that he will become worthless for even worldly good. Without intervention, all victims will die in their stupefied states. The only antidote to cure a victim from irreversible harm is a healthy dose of...you guessed it...heavenly love.

You were indeed made to be a lover of people. Do you recall in a previous lesson when we told you that you "wield a great and wonderful strength"? We hope that you did not think we were referring to the elasticity of your trouser straps. "Young men...you are strong," says the great apostle John! And in case you need reminding, this strength comes from the love manifest in you by Jesus Christ, if you indeed equate yourself with His calling.

We emphasize that the qualities of love do not include emotional feelings so much as they include commitment and resolve. We stated such in "Made for Marriage," and we do so again here. Oh, young man, that you would remember this truth above else!

Perhaps these Scriptures will help solidify in you a proper frame of mind:

> *A new commandment I give to you, that you love one another, even as I have loved you...* *John 13:34*

> *Greater love has no one than this, that one lay down his life for his friends.* *John 15:13*

For God so loved the world, that He gave His only begotten Son, that whoever believes in Him shall not perish, but have eternal life.   *John 3:16*

"Love bears all things, believes all things, upholds all things..." says the great thirteenth chapter of First Corinthians. The world's largest crane or excavator cannot uphold all things, but love can! We implore you to be a lover of your fellow man. If you have never done so, pray this simple prayer with sincerity: "Dear Lord, help me to love my fellow man with all that I have. I offer myself to You for this very cause...."

Patience

Have you ever wondered where the phrase "patience is a virtue" comes from? Patience is indeed a virtue, and we hope to help explain why it is so, along with a few of the benefits from having it.

For one, patience is the kind of thing that will reduce the stress load that one might otherwise carry. Who wants to walk around stressed most of the time? Not me! And neither should you.

Now we are not talking about the feeling that might be generated when you and a friend are attempting to mow several large lawns in one day. It's natural and useful for you to feel a certain amount of anxiety when you are cutting turf in this fashion. But how might you act when things don't go according to your timetable?

Suppose you run out of gas and your partner has to bike a half mile to fetch more fuel. Might you get stressed and irritable, wishing your friend could fly? We hope not, but this is how an impatient man may behave.

Or suppose you are waiting at a fast food counter, having

already ordered and paid for your meal. What might you do if you were to see that others who were behind you have already been served and are now seated, while you are still waiting? Might you pitch a fit? We hope not, but more than one man has unraveled a counter girl's pigtails simply because he was impatient.

In the grand scheme of things, an impatient temperament does not help to get anything done faster or better. No act of road rage ever made a wider lane. No tapping of a foot ever made paint dry faster. And no amount of pacing ever made the sun set sooner. More importantly, no amount of impatience ever procured an answered prayer before its intended time.

An impatient man will think himself the victim, for the earth spins at never the right speed. How futile and silly such a man appears, one moment braced against a mountain's wall to slow the great, blue marble's roll, the next running frantically across the plains like a gerbil in an exercise wheel, affecting no other spin but his own.

Patience is universally useful. For one thing, a patient man can be trusted by others. Why should an impatient man expect others to have faith in him, knowing that his exposed nerves might short circuit the moment something touched him off? However, a patient man communicates to others that he is safe, and they will be more prone to trust and believe in him.

Consider the farmer, who, not knowing if it shall rain or shine, puts his hand to the plow, fertilizes the soil, plants his seed, and patiently waits for the results. Is he not many times more commendable than the man who shouts at the sky, demanding rain one day, sun the next?

Consider also the great Farmer, the Vinedresser, the Husbandman of the vineyard. Is He not supremely patient with us, His branches? Of course He is. Let us be patient then likewise, so that we may bear much fruit for His glory!

Kindness

Of all the manifestations of the Spirit, kindness must be ranked as one of the easiest to employ. How difficult is it, really, to provide a kind word, or to perform an act of charitable service? It is easy indeed, and so kindness should flow from us as easily as water flows down a mountain stream.

A word of kindness is like a seed, which dropped by chance, produces in time a wildflower worthy of its place in heaven's bouquet. A kind word is not only a precursor to life, it is life itself, for the Scriptures are clear that "Death and life are in the power of the tongue, and those who love it will eat its fruit" (Prov. 18:21).

Listen intently to those who speak, so that when it is time to respond you might let them know that *they have been heard*, and thus they will be enabled to properly engage throughout the course of further conversation. How might you do this? For one thing, you might study those who do this naturally. We promise you that no one will fault you for copying him. You will find, in your study of such people, that they commonly repeat what was spoken, or that they ask questions to get clarification. Talking with people in this manner is a true act of kindness.

Of course, kindness also involves giving compliments. Be lavish in your praise for others. It is doubtful that you will need to back off from doing this too much. It has been said that one of the driving motivations within humans is the need to feel appreciated. If this is so, how awful it is to withhold appreciation from someone when it is due, especially when it costs nothing to give it. When someone does something worthy of your appreciation, then let your kindness flow! At the bare minimum, offer your thanks, but it may be more appropriate to put into words what you are thankful for.

However, avoid flattery, which is giving someone a compliment that is either undeserved or not heartfelt. If you start sounding sappy and insincere, we hope that a good friend will let you know it! The Bible does not have anything kind to say about flattery.

You should know that words of kindness must not always include complimentary language. Suppose you were caught unawares with your zipper down or your shoes untied. Would it not be a kind gesture if someone told you of your shortcoming in a discreet manner? Of course it would. But too many people are afraid of offending others when telling them the truth for their own good. However, kindness should never be used as a license to be tongue-tied when someone is in a serious predicament.

Kindness is not confined to the realm of words. Offering your seat to another, paying someone else's expense, or cleaning a hunting buddy's quota of game birds are just a few of the many acts of charity you can offer your fellow man. A caution regarding acts of charity, however: don't reserve your good deeds for only those who might somehow repay you. On the contrary, include your acts of kindness toward those who may never repay you, and even for the undeserving. Such is the way of our Lord.

Goodness

We might say that God is everything the devil is not, but in doing so we fall far short of fully describing God. The same is true for goodness. Goodness is everything badness is not, but a simple contrast in this regard might leave goodness shortchanged.

To do good means to have a good heart. Do you want to do well? If so, you are more than halfway to meeting your end, for as a vinedresser plans to cultivate his yard, so do good intentions precede benevolence. Beware, however, for as the saying goes, "The road to hell is paved with good intentions." A man of goodness follows through with his intentions, but to him following through is not an afterthought. Rather, intentions and doing are one in the same.

Goodness and godliness go hand-in-hand. In fact, doing good is what Jesus is all about. While on earth, He spoke good news, made the lame to walk, and the blind to see. You, too, can carry on His good work. There are many good men already doing so, and you are slated to join them!

A man with a good heart is easy to recognize. Such a man professes Christ in both word and deed. He is rarely in a hurry. He smiles often, and his listening ear precedes his good word. He is the kind of man that might be taken advantage of, if his good heart were not guarded well. Pity the fool who attempts such advantage, for heaven will pay him appropriate recompense. The Lord watches over a good heart with special interest, like a winemaker who guards a special variety of grapes of great worth.

A man with a good heart is well spoken of, more so than others but not by all, for a good man knows the futility of attempting universal approval. When spoken of unfavorably, a goodhearted man may be pained, but only momentarily, for there is a self-comforting quality in goodness, although a good man may be too humble to recognize it in these terms.

A goodhearted man, advanced in age, is the pinnacle object of admiration of every boy who never had his own grandfather. Ah, to sit on the lap of such a man, to hear tales of war and peace, to learn at his side in the woodshop and afield, to be inspired, and to do great things as this man did…. Do you have a grandfather that emulates godliness? If so, we implore you to make it your life's aim to one day be like him. If not, we encourage you to become such a man for the sake of your progeny and for the many other lives you will touch along the way.

Goodness, a supreme virtue, nonetheless cannot stand alone. Acts of charity and benevolence, apart from God, are useful only in temporal terms. For as the Scripture states, many do-gooders will cite their good works before Christ at Judgment, at which time He will state to certain men, "I never knew you...."

Faithfulness

Essentially, faithfulness is remaining committed to a cause. For example, a farmer must persevere throughout the entire sowing and reaping process; he can't give up simply because he gets tired or is worried about the seasonal forecast. Even if his plough ox is rustled or his wagon breaks an axle, he will need to remain faithful to his cause, especially if he has already begun his endeavor.

Likewise, a vinedresser must be faithful throughout the entire course of overseeing his vineyard. He must be constantly aware of the condition of his soil and his vines. If foxes or raccoons are frequenting his vineyard, he must set traps or hire bounty hunters to rid of them. He must plan his harvest carefully, for the amount of sugar found in his clusters is contingent upon careful timing. The pressed juices must be stored just-so in order to achieve his desired effect. In short, he must be a faithful student and administrator of his craft.

In these examples, the stewards were committed to a cause that they had already begun. Failure on their part to carry out some or all of their duties would seriously affect the outcome of their efforts. But does this mean that you must always be faithful, even in "lost causes"? This is a very good question, for which there is no universal answer. You may, in fact, endeavor upon a cause and find that you wish you hadn't. In this scenario, you must be faithful in the grand scheme of things. It may be that bailing out is the best thing to do for the overall good. A good rule of thumb is to determine if you would be putting anyone out by your actions. Remember the Golden Rule, and do your best to abide by it.

A discussion on faithfulness would not be complete without pointing out the importance of keeping your word. A person's word is usually the first thing heard and processed by others before any action is carried out. So if you say you are going to do something, then be good on your word.

Do you hope to have much responsibility some day? Regardless of whether or not you want to become an ice cream truck driver, a dog catcher, an astronaut, or a brain surgeon, you will need to start practicing responsibility now. You should know that Jesus taught, "He who is faithful in a very little thing is faithful also in much" (Luke 16:10). So you can do your part of helping the Spirit's fruit to grow by being faithful with small things. This means you should be consistently putting your bike away before you ask for your dad's car keys, and gladly eating what was provided at lunch before requesting New York strip sirloin for dinner.

Faithfulness as it pertains to the Spirit's fruit goes far beyond being a good steward of things. In terms of commitment toward a cause, the Spirit's fruit demonstrates your willingness and ability to *keep the faith*. The Scriptures indicate that this is not something to take for granted, nor something you should consider lightly. The apostle Paul proudly stated near the end of his life, "...the time of my departure has come. I have fought the good fight, I have finished the course, I have kept the faith" (2 Tim. 4:6-7).

When you are old and gray, will be able to say, as Paul did, that you kept the faith? We trust that you will. But understand this: your faith *must be your own!* Perhaps it already is, and if so, we join in heaven's applause. Yet many a young man's faith was started by the imparting of his parents' faith upon him, and so each boy must eventually wean himself from his parents' faith so that he can realize his own as a man. He must, in essence, transform from flower to fruit.

Can you honestly say that your faith is your own and not your parents' or somebody else's? God forbid, but what if your parents should die? Such a question should not frighten you, though it may give you pause. Would you, could you, carry on? We're not merely asking if you could survive; we're confident enough that you could round up enough scraps to see you through. Rather, we're asking this: could you, with conviction and effectiveness, fight the good fight, and run the good race, and keep the good faith, *on your own...without turning back?*

Gentleness

We would not be surprised if the idea of being gentle does not instantly appeal to you. After all, the idea of being gentle often conjures up images of being dainty, soft spoken, or overly careful. For many people, gentleness seems reserved for the effeminate. But rest assured, the kind of gentleness that the Scriptures refer to is very much in line with being a man.

Perhaps it is best to start off by describing what gentleness is not. Gentleness is not the opposite of being assertive. We know this to be true because Jesus was very much assertive and was in fact so most of the time. Do you have the ability and willingness to take the lead when no one better than you can, or the ability to instantly follow when the opportunity calls for it? If so, then you are being assertive, and that is a good thing. You do not have to be dainty about leading or following. We hope this helps bring clarification.

So what, then, is gentleness? You already know that being a Christian means that you wield a great and wonderful strength. Among other things, gentleness means exercising your strength with sincere humility so that others might be served. For example, if you are a big brother, you should not order your younger siblings around just because you think yourself privileged.

A gentle man knows that boasting will usually bruise the Spirit's fruit, rather than keep it ripe and fresh. Can you bench press more than your own body weight or jump five garbage cans with your bike? If so, good for you, but you better be careful showing off to others who can't. In all regards, keep your pride in check. Such is the way of a gentle man.

Are we saying that gentleness involves holding back your muscles? In some cases it might, but we are not saying that you should hold back in all cases. Let's discuss a hypothetical situation to help clarify: Suppose you were an accomplished wrestler, having won several dual meets with very few losses, and you now have an opportunity to show a friend a few moves. Are you going to instantly put him in fireman's carry, followed by a painful cross-face cradle, just because you can? We hope not! You will not have taught him anything other than how to show off and that he should avoid any future instruction from you.

But what if you are in direct competition with others near your equal? Should you hold back then? Not on your life! Show your stuff, or you will be shown up!

Suppose you are in a fully uniformed football game, playing middle linebacker. Being gentle in spirit does not mean you should tiptoe toward the ball carrier and first ask his permission to tackle him. On the contrary, hit him, man, full speed! Make him think twice about running your way again.

But what if, after hitting him, *you* are the man down, and he is on his way to further yardage? Are you going to cower in deference, all in the name of "gentleness"? We hope not! Next time, meet him harder, faster, and altogether better, so that it is he who goes down rather than you.

Competition provides an opportunity for kindness, for it is kind to help hone the skills of another by offering him your best effort. At the end of a game, however, a gentle man will be a good sport. If you win, don't gloat. If you lose, don't pout. That pretty much sums up what being a good sport is all about.

A discussion on this topic would be incomplete if we did not point out that a gentle man knows how and when to be a gentleman. A gentleman is polite when the occasion calls for it, which is often. If you have mastered "please," "thank you," and "you're welcome," you are over halfway to being a gentleman. But there is more to being a gentleman than offering verbal courtesies. We encourage you to review our lesson entitled "Social Skills" if the finer points of manners and etiquette elude you.

Perhaps the best measure of one's ability to exercise gentleness can be found in his speech. The Bible has a lot to say about how we should exercise language. Here are just some of the many passages associated with this topic:

A gentle answer turns away wrath, but a harsh word stirs up anger.   *Prov. 15:1*

...Speak truth each one of you with his neighbor, for we are members of one another.... Let no unwholesome word proceed from your mouth, but only such a word as is good for edification according to the need of the moment, so that it will give grace to those who hear.   *Eph. 4:25, 29*

This you know, my beloved brethren. But everyone must be quick to hear, slow to speak and slow to anger.   *James 1:19*

...For the mouth speaks out of that which fills the heart.   *Matt. 12:34*

230 • Made for Manhood

Self-Control

It is a true statement that a man is not really able to control anybody other than himself. Certainly, we are able to *influence* others, but we cannot truly control them. There are too many variables which prevent it, the chief one being the fact that God created men with a free will.

Everybody has a free will. What does this mean? It means that we are able to exercise many options in our lives, both small and large. You and I are free to put our left sock on before our right one as a matter of routine, if we so want. If we want to change this habit and put our right one on first, we may do so. Likewise, we are able to make choices in more important matters of life, like what kind of gun we might save up for, or whether or not we will go to college.

To be sure, there are certain things about ourselves that we cannot control at all, and others we can control, but only to a degree. For example, we have no control over the rate at which our hair grows, nor can we swallow and breathe at exactly the same time. And once our noses decide to sneeze, we can only hold off doing so for so long. Likewise, we may be able to refrain from blinking for a few minutes, but sooner or later our eyelids will dominate our wills.

You may have noticed in your Bible reading that the Scriptures don't really have much to say about what sock you put on first or what kind of gun you might save up for or how long you can go without blinking. This is so because God is far more concerned with your character than He is about anything else. He knows that you have a free will, and that you can use your free will to make good choices or evil choices. So of course God wants you to exercise self-control in this regard.

As a young man growing toward Christian maturity, it is vital to know that you have complete control over choosing evil.

Here are a couple of passages to help solidify this important point:

> *No temptation has overtaken you but such as is common to man; and God is faithful, who will not allow you to be tempted beyond what you are able, but with the temptation will provide the way of escape also, so that you will be able to endure it.*   *1 Cor. 10:13*

> *...knowing this, that our old self was crucified with Him, in order that our body of sin might be done away with, so that we would no longer be slaves to sin; for he who has died is freed from sin....Even so consider yourselves to be dead to sin, but alive to God in Christ Jesus.*   *Rom. 6:7, 11*

> *My little children, I am writing these things to you so that you may not sin...*   *1 John 2:1*

Indeed, the Bible has a lot to say about the subject of sin. It's sad to say, but there are some well meaning (and some not so well meaning) teachers of the Bible who really cloud this matter. Some of these teachers falsely purport that Christians will always live a defeated life of sin, not being able to do otherwise. This teaching is rooted in the false worldview that mankind does not really have a free will. But how could the Bible state that self-control is part of the Holy Spirit's fruit if it were not possible to control oneself? The idea is just ridiculous. We would encourage you to avoid teachings that imply that a victorious life is not normal, and to respectfully correct such a teaching after recognizing it.

We have previously discussed the importance of being faithful in small things before being faithful in large. This principle applies to all matters in life, self-control not withstanding. So we encourage you to purposefully make it your life's aim to exercise self-control with small things; doing so will help you when real temptation comes your way.

What do we mean by exercising self-control in small things? We really have no set prescription, but we do recommend a concerted effort to *live a disciplined life*. This might mean simply controlling the urge to laugh out loud in a public library, or refraining from buying a new bike just because your old one has a few loose spokes. A disciplined life might include not sleeping in, or developing an efficient routine of carrying out chores and study. Sooner or later, rest assured, you will face even weightier matters, and being a disciplined man will equip you to meet with success.

How More Fruit is Made

As a young man, you should naturally aspire to bear fruit for Christ's kingdom. So you should know a bit about how God grows His fruit.

Earlier in our lesson, we cited the biblical passage in which Jesus describes our Father as the owner of the vineyard, Himself as the vine, and His followers as branches. To this effect He stated, "Every branch in Me that does not bear fruit, He takes away; and every branch that bears fruit, He prunes it so that it may bear more fruit…" (John 15:2).

One of the key ways that God produces fruit is to remove fruitless branches from the vine. While this may be startling in its implications, it really should not be that surprising. Any good gardener or horticulturist knows that a branch that is not producing fruit is nevertheless using certain nutrients at the expense of the branches that are fruitful. So the best thing a caretaker can do for the overall good of the plant is to completely get rid of branches that are not producing any fruit. Such branches are good for nothing other than firewood.

However, many branches bear fruit as intended. This is where the skill of a good caretaker really comes in. A person with such skill knows that certain parts of the branches sometimes need to be removed so that the plant can grow the way the caretaker wants. For example, a vinedresser may want to improve the health of certain grapes, so he may choose to cut off specific leaves so that more sunshine can reach previously concealed areas. Or the vinedresser may cut off parts of a branch that are diseased so that the surrounding areas will not be adversely affected.

In like fashion, God "prunes" us, in that He removes certain things in our lives so that we can grow the way He wants us to. How will He do this in your life? Ah, that is a question we are not equipped to answer, at least not fully. Maybe it will involve removing something that causes you grief so that you can be healthy, or it may be that He will allow a trial or a tribulation to occur in your life so that you can be tested and thus be bettered (James 1:3).

Regardless of how God works to cause you to grow, know that you are in good hands. He is the supreme Vinedresser, the Husbandman, the Master Gardener. He knows exactly what you need to make you bear fruit for His glory. Therefore, be ever aware that no matter what happens in your life, God can cause it to work for the good to cause you to become more like Jesus!

Being a Man of Conviction

We are now near the end of our lessons, at least as far as this book is concerned. So how shall we conclude? We could finish by describing some of the cool adventures that may be in store. Or we might end by describing some of the trials and tribulations that await you, for you will surely be tested with what you now know. The former might make for an exciting prelude to the rest of your life; the latter might cause you to wonder if you are ready for it all.

So how shall we end our study for this time being? We will indulge by assuming you are ready for it all, that we can load you with anticipation of anything that may await you. But in doing so, we will equip you with ample admonishment appropriate for your present and future hour.

A Real Man

You cannot appropriately resume your present hour nor move into the future without determining to be a real man. Perhaps you have already done this months or years ago, and if so we applaud you. But you must know, and we mean *really know*, what it means to be a real man.

For one thing, a real man is one who *has strong convictions*.

Too many men are unfamiliar with this concept, for we live in a world whereby strong convictions are often frowned upon. Being a man of conviction means you know what you believe, and you believe what you know. And everything you believe and know is exemplified in your life.

Passion and Truth

As a man of conviction, you will be able to readily identify truth, and you will love it more than anything else. Conversely, you will be able to identify falsehood and thus hate it. You will love the truth so much that you will be forever willing to both live and die for it, and you will hate the lie so much that you will forever want its demise.

The promotion of partial truth brings only fractional satisfaction to the man of conviction, and in fact he may be more frustrated than satisfied whenever the whole of truth is withheld. Likewise,merely silencing the lie will leave the man of conviction only partially relieved. Rather, he can find rest and rejoice only when the lie breathes no longer.

The man of conviction takes refuge in the whole of God's Word, but a passage he holds especially dear is the proclamation of Jesus when He said, "I am the way, the truth, and the life..." (John 14:6).

The man of conviction is also one who *feels*, and often he will do so deeply. Whether it be joy, sorrow, righteous indignation, or any other passion, a real man is able and willing to express his heart in a manner that tells the world that Jesus lives in and through him.

Lastly, a real man does not try to be anybody else but himself. His convictions are simply too strong to consider otherwise. While he may encounter other men he would like to emulate, he does so only to the degree that it honors them. Rather, he remains at ease knowing that God is at work guiding and raising him as He sees fit.

Worldview, Foundations, and Conviction

In a previous lesson, we discussed the importance of having a proper worldview. We will elaborate on its importance here and its relevance to godly conviction:

A proper worldview is like a solid foundation. A foundation, in case you didn't know, is the base upon which any building structure is built. Your house has a foundation which is likely made of concrete, blocks, stone, or timbers. A good foundation allows a house to be stable; a poor one might cause the home to shift and become out of level and thus crack.

Jesus said that anyone who built his life upon His teachings was like a man who built a house on a firm foundation. He stated,

> *Therefore, everyone who hears these words of Mine and acts on them, may be compared to a wise man who built his house on the rock. And the rain fell, and the floods came, and the winds blew and slammed against that house; and yet it did not fall, for it had been founded on the rock. Everyone who hears these words of Mine and does not act on them, will be like a foolish man who built his house on the sand. The rain fell, and the floods came, and the winds blew and slammed against that house; and it fell—and great was its fall.*
> *Matt. 7:24-28*

Conviction can be compared to the bonding agent in a foundation. For example, the bonding agent in a concrete block foundation is cement. The cement itself is made of water, fine limestone, and mason sand with possibly some mortar added. If the cement is not mixed, applied, and allowed to cure properly, the foundation system will be compromised.

Suppose a man constructing a block foundation had too much sand and not enough water in one of his batches of cement mix, though the rest of his batches were mixed properly. Most of his foundation might be sound, but the area that was constructed with faulty cement would have weak, crumbly joints. Would this cause the whole house to fall? Probably not, but the owner might discover a nasty crack in his basement or elsewhere above the faulty area. Likewise, a man lacking proper conviction might encounter difficulty during his life because of his lack.

Now consider another man building a different block foundation. This man's problems are even greater, for he completely forgot to order the necessary components to make his cement. In an attempt to improvise, he uses water from a mud puddle instead of clean water, debris-laden dirt from a ditch in lieu of filtered mason sand, and a large bag of flour that was intended for his wife's pantry in place of fine limestone. As you might suspect, this man's foundation is utterly doomed to fail! But this is what it is like for the man who understands a proper worldview but has no depth of conviction to implement it. So you can see that a man's ability to build his life upon a firm foundation is proportional to the strength of his conviction.

How much better it is for the man who constructs his block foundation using proper components and methods! This man has a solid base on which to build the rest of his home so that it will stay plumb and level for the long haul. He is, as Jesus stated, the "wise man who built his house on the rock."

The Importance of Virtue

A real man also possesses the necessary virtues to make his convictions sensible and useful. A man might embrace a proper worldview, but be too prideful or selfish when demonstrating it. Or, a man might be too chicken or aloof to properly let others know what he believed. Two important virtues essential to being a man of conviction are *integrity* and *resolve*. Integrity and resolve go hand-in-hand as much as any two virtues can. Let's discuss integrity first.

Integrity

Integrity is a firm adherence to a set of standards. Sometimes this set of standards is referred to as a "code." A man with integrity holds his standards close to heart; they are as important to him as life itself. As a Christian, your set of standards is the "Golden Rule," which can be summed up as loving God with all your heart and doing to others as you would have done to you.

A man with integrity does the right thing no matter what the circumstance. In this regard, such a man is said to maintain a high code of *ethics*. Some people might be willing to do the right thing as long as others can see them doing so, but a real man does the right thing even when nobody is looking. He doesn't care if others see him, for doing good is his chief aim.

Consider the young farmhand who sets off to demonstrate just how much fun he can have when his boss is not around. Not being seen, he spends passing moments now and again in the loft, throwing rocks at the pigeons and drinking fresh milk he has stolen from the cow. He has deduced that whenever the chickens begin to cluck and clatter just so, a sure sign has been given that the boss is coming around to check on things. Ever on guard for the chickens' signal, the boy remains poised to reposition himself as though he has been working.

Days, weeks, and even months go by in this fashion. This boy, regularly being paid for all his reported time, has successfully fashioned for himself a double life. He appears virtuous and dutiful, but only when seen. Is this boy a model of integrity? Hah! Not on your life.

Exercising integrity is altogether beneficial. For one thing, a man with integrity never has to worry about getting caught because he doesn't have anything to hide. But more important, society is perpetually bettered by his presence, for integrity bears its own offspring: charity, honesty, protector, and a help-in-time-of-need are some of their many names.

Concerning integrity, T.L. Haines wrote, "The world is always asking for men who are not for sale; men who are honest, sound from the center to circumference, true to the heart's core; men who will condemn wrong in friend or foe, in themselves as well as others…men who will stand for the right if the heavens totter and the earth reels; men who can tell the truth, and look the world and the devil right in the eye…who will not fail nor be discouraged till judgment be set in the earth." Do you aspire to be such a man? If so, we commend you, and we pronounce you well on your way if you are not in fact so already.

Resolve

Resolve involves *firmness of purpose*. A man with resolve knows what he wants to do and fixes his sight and efforts on accomplishing his intent. He may or may not meet his aim immediately, but regardless he is never swayed, for he knows that in due time resolve will have its way.

You might think that resolve and patience are somewhat similar, and if so you are right. But resolve is more than patience. Patience demonstrates an appropriate *reaction* by way of tolerance and forbearance. Conversely, a man of resolve knows matter-of-factly that "in this world ye shall have tribulation," and so is *proactive* in that his character is conditioned to resist, endure, and overcome whatever comes his way, no matter what the cost.

Conviction and Influence

A man of conviction has the potential to powerfully influence others if he puts his convictions into action. If his convictions are sound, being based upon a proper worldview, then his influence can be used for the good. However, if he embraces a faulty worldview, his conclusions about how things should be done in the world might produce a bad influence.

Imagine a group of sociologists who, upon exercising their strong convictions, convince the public that fresh air and sunshine are not healthy and that humans are better off sleeping by day and interacting by night. Or consider a party of politicians who convincingly declare that Bibles can only be published in pig Latin and sold only after a five hundred percent sales tax was imposed. Are these suppositions absurd? Indeed, they are. But not much more so than some of the ridiculous ideas that our culture has embraced from various men of influence. Many of these ideas can easily be traced to a faulty worldview.

Thankfully, there are many thousands of examples of men who have proper worldviews with strong convictions and who have influenced the world for good. You would do well to study the lives of such men as Moses, the apostle Paul, and others throughout history who have represented Christ well. And to be sure, you probably don't have to look much further than your own father and many of his friends for godly examples.

A Certain Grip

The man of conviction embraces an appropriate degree of certainty in regard to his convictions. He knows the importance of being immovable on certain matters, but he knows also that he does not own the last word on all that is said in regard to truth. He is keenly aware of the Scripture that says, "For now we see in a mirror dimly, but then face to face; now I know in part, but then I will know fully just as I also have been fully known" (1 Cor. 13:12).

It is a sure thing that you will never know all there is to know on any matter, nor will your pastor, your father, or any of your neighbors. Not even Oprah, Kid Rock, and Al Gore combined have complete knowledge of any topic, regardless of how popular and convincing they might be.

However, you can still know something *truly* even though you may not know it *exhaustively*. You do not need to be wishy-washy about your beliefs, and in fact it is wrong for you to be so. We counsel you to be certain to the degree you are so, and to humbly admit your lack of knowledge when appropriate. This is the way of a teachable spirit. A man of conviction is always prepared to consider that he may have something more to learn about a matter.

Admitting Lack

Consider the passage in Acts which describes Apollos as "...an eloquent man, ...mighty in the Scriptures. This man had been instructed in the way of the Lord; and being fervent in spirit, he was speaking and *teaching accurately* the things concerning Jesus...But when Priscilla and Aquila heard him, they took him aside and *explained to him the way of God more accurately*" (18:24-26, emphasis added).

Apollos was a man who was "teaching accurately" but was further instructed by others so that he knew his subject matter "more accurately." If this eloquent, fervent, and otherwise accurate man learned from fellow Christians so as to improve his knowledge, so can you. You will do well to keep an open mind to the fact that you don't know everything.

In your life, it is likely you will read and hear many different ideas in the way of various disciplines, such as theology, politics, sociology, and business. Don't be surprised if sound logic leads you to conclude that some of these ideas are more accurate and valid than your previously held ones, and it may be best that you embrace them. Such is the way of learning. But you will never be a good learner if you think that you already know your subject matter fully.

The Non-Negotiables

It is vital that you understand the importance of having a teachable spirit. But it is even more vital that you understand the importance of being unshakable in the *tenets of your faith.*

The tenets of your faith are those parts essential to maintaining the integrity of your faith. For example, we know that Jesus was a real man who lived on earth at a real time in history, and that He made certain, real claims that cannot be misunderstood. Among other things, He claimed to be the Son of God and the only way to knowing God. He stated that only through Him could forgiveness of sins be realized, and that eternal life would be granted for those who believe on His holy name. These truths are as certain as the fact that you are alive and reading these words; no amount of arguing or persuasive thought should ever make you believe otherwise.

The integrity of a man's faith is compromised, and in many cases destroyed, when the tenets of his faith are abandoned. Why is this so important to realize? To be sure, many slick talkers will attempt to convince you that various falsehoods are true, and that the truth you embrace is false. The Bible is replete with warnings in this regard:

> *For many deceivers have gone out into the world, those who do not acknowledge Jesus Christ as coming in the flesh. This is the deceiver and the antichrist.*
> *2 John 1:7*

> *If anyone advocates a different doctrine and does not*
> *agree with sound words, those of our Lord Jesus Christ,*
> *and with the doctrine conforming to godliness, he is*
> *conceited and understands nothing...*   *1 Tim. 6:3-4*

> *...be on your guard so that you are not carried away*
> *by the error of unprincipled men and fall from your own*
> *steadfastness, but grow in the grace and knowledge of*
> *our Lord and Savior Jesus Christ.*   *2 Pet. 3:17-18*

So if a smooth talker should try to convince you that Jesus was a sinner, or that the Bible cannot be trusted, or that you evolved from monkeys, or that aliens are coming to take you to heaven, or any other teaching that is against sound, biblical reason, you would do well to stand your ground.

A Doer of the Word

We have already discussed the importance of embracing a proper worldview and having appropriate virtues so that your convictions can be sensible and useful. But as you likely know, these qualities are not the only things needed.

As a man of conviction, you will also need to be a "doer of the word." Here's what the book of James has to say about this particular subject:

> *But prove yourselves doers of the word, and not*
> *merely hearers who delude themselves. For if anyone*
> *is a hearer of the word and not a doer, he is like a man*
> *who looks at his natural face in a mirror; for once he*
> *has looked at himself and gone away, he has immediately*
> *forgotten what kind of person he was. But one who*
> *looks intently at the perfect law, the law of liberty, and*
> *abides by it, not having become a forgetful hearer but an*
> *effectual doer, this man will be blessed in what he does.*
> *James 1:22-25*

A doer of the word is one who puts his faith into action. He is not content to listen to a good sermon and merely say "Amen" to the things that sound good to him. Nor is he content in reading books about the faith of other men. Rather, he employs his faith by loving God and others. He practices the kind of faith that James describes as such: "Pure and undefiled religion in the sight of our God and Father is this: to visit orphans and widows in their distress, and to keep oneself unstained by the world" (1:27).

Hypocrisy

The opposite of a doer of the word is a *hypocrite*. A hypocrite is someone who puts on a false appearance of virtue or religion. Jesus condemned many of the religious leaders of His day by saying, "But woe to you, scribes and Pharisees, hypocrites, because you shut off the kingdom of heaven from people; for you do not enter in yourselves, nor do you allow those who are entering to go in." Jesus called these men several pointed names in His rebukes, among them being "blind guides," "serpents," "brood of vipers," and "whitewashed tombs" (Matt. 23:13-27). Needless to say, Jesus does not take kindly to hypocrisy.

We should all be on guard for the possibility of committing hypocrisy, for this vice takes many forms. Often, hypocrisy can simply involve acting in contradiction to one's stated beliefs. For example, a man may declare to others that going to the movies is wrong, even though that same man watches various sit-coms at home on his television. Or a man may declare that hunting is wrong, even though he sets mouse traps and sprays bug killer. Perhaps another man declares that smoking is sinful due to its ill side effects, even though this same man regularly drinks Mountain Dew instead of water. A case might be made that such men are committing hypocrisy, for their stated beliefs are not entirely consistent with their behaviors.

There are a number of sensible ways to guard against

hypocrisy. For one thing, be very careful about condemning the behaviors of others, especially when you are not privy to another man's heart condition.

Similarly, you should be cautious about universally condemning behaviors the Bible is not entirely clear about. Truth be told, the Bible does not say anything directly about television, ridding of pests, or Mountain Dew. To be sure, the Bible does condemn specific behaviors, but often God leaves certain judgments up to us. Do you remember the passage in James regarding being a doer of the word? According to that passage, the "perfect law" that we are to abide in is the *"law of liberty"* (1:25). Indeed, the New Testament is replete with its admonishment to avoid declaring how everyone should behave in all circumstances.

Judging Others

We will get right to the point in identifying a common misconception in regard to this topic. Too many Christians falsely state that it is wrong to judge others. "Judge not," you will hear them say, often with a sufficient air of conviction to make others think that is all the Bible has to say on the matter. But such people are either misinformed or shortchanged in their own convictions, for they neglect the whole of the Bible on this subject, and in doing so they discredit the true admonishment of Jesus and His apostles.

In fact, God expects us to exercise sound judgment, but in doing so He also provides ample warning. Consider a key passage on this subject:

> *"Do not judge so that you will not be judged. For in the way you judge, you will be judged; and by your standard of measure, it will be measured to you. Why do you look at the speck that is in your brother's eye, but do not notice the log that is in your own eye? Or how*

can you say to your brother, 'Let me take the speck out
of your eye,' and behold, the log is in your own eye?
You hypocrite, first take the log out of your own eye, and
then you will see clearly to take the speck out of your
brother's eye."   *Matt. 7:1-5*

The heart of Jesus' concern is for us to avoid hypocrisy. If we do judge, we should expect the same measure of judgment in return. But are we to remain silent if we see a brother with something in his eye? Of course not, for even the smallest foreign object can lead to infection and possible blindness. Rather, it is evident that Jesus wants us to "see clearly" so that we can properly judge the condition of a brother who has something in his eye. And we can make certain of our ability to see clearly by making sure we don't have anything in our own eyes.

Does the Bible ever directly admonish us to judge? This is a very important and legitimate question. Consider the following passage in response to this question:

I wrote you in my letter not to associate with immoral
people; I did not at all mean with the immoral people
of this world, or with the covetous and swindlers, or
with idolaters, for then you would have to go out of
the world. But actually, I wrote to you not to associate
with any so-called brother if he is an immoral person,
or covetous, or an idolater, or a reviler, or a drunkard,
or a swindler—not even to eat with such a one. For
what have I to do with judging outsiders? Do you not
judge those who are within the church? But those who
are outside, God judges. Remove the wicked one from
among yourselves.   *Cor. 5:9-13*

This passage clearly tells us to exercise sound judgment in regard to "so-called brothers," indicating that it is possible that certain people in church might claim to be Christians but in fact are not, evidenced by what appears to be unrepentant, chronic, and overt sin. In fact, we are not to even associate with such people. Why is this so? It is likely that associating with a so-called Christian who is unrepentant will only enable him to continue in his folly, and in the meantime be the possible cause for true believers to be led astray.

Convictions and Stumbling Blocks

You can do your part to avoid unintentional tension by not flaunting certain convictions in front of other Christians who cannot appreciate them. For example, a father and son might share the conviction that hunting is a God-given sport which is best started at an early age. If this be the case, the son should refrain from sharing with certain friends that he shot an eight point buck, if he knows that those friends are not allowed to do likewise. Or perhaps a boy's mother allows him to occasionally drink coffee, but his friend's mother thinks that doing so at a young age is wrong. Sharing the fact that he can drink coffee might cause his friend to "stumble" in his Christian walk. Such a friend might be tempted to become jealous, or to question his parents' convictions at too early an age to be beneficial to him.

The bottom line is that you want to be careful of sharing or demonstrating your convictions if it will cause someone weak in the faith to stumble or otherwise sin. Your parents will give you sufficient guidance if ever you should need clarification in regard to specific situations.

The Myth of Offense

There has been a longstanding trend among certain churches to emphasize the importance of never offending people. We resist this trend, for it does not stand up to sound, biblical reason. In truth, these churches lack a certain degree of conviction, and so we hope to bring a balance to this very important topic here.

Before we begin, let us first clarify something: We are *not* suggesting that you should go out of your way to *try* to offend others. But neither should you be afraid of doing so, especially when it comes to verbally sharing your faith. Nor are we saying that feelings are unimportant. We should consider them and be careful when choosing our words. But too many Christians are obsessed with protecting the feelings of others, and in truth they need not be.

Jesus was certainly not overly concerned with the feelings of others, for he placed a greater value on their souls than He did their feelings. To the young rich young ruler, He said, "If you wish to be complete, go and sell your possessions and give to the poor, and you will have treasure in heaven; and come, follow Me." If you remember the story, you know the young man walked away offended (Matt. 19:21).

Jesus gave reason for the woman at the well to be embarrassed (John 4:17-18); to the healed blind man He said, "...do not sin any more, so that nothing worse may befall you" (John 5:14); He ordered Peter to "get behind Me Satan" (Matt. 16:40). He told a man who wanted to follow Him to "let the dead bury their own dead" (Matt. 8:22). He informed a crowd that was following Him that they could not be His disciples unless they "hated" others (Luke 14:25-26); and so on....

Perhaps Jesus best summed up the issue of offense when He stated that He came to divide (Matt. 10:34). It's no wonder the Bible refers to Jesus as "A stone of stumbling and a rock of offense" (Isa. 8:14, 1 Pet. 2:8, Rom. 9:33). If these passages make some Christians uncomfortable, it is because they do not see the liberating effect they have when received.

Sharing Your Convictions

Now we have come to perhaps the most vital part of this lesson, and that is the importance of sharing your convictions with others. We have already discussed the importance of being a doer of the word, for faith without works is dead. But a man who promotes good deeds without sharing his faith with others shortchanges everyone involved.

What can we liken such a man to? He is like a sealed Cracker Jack box with the world's best prize trapped in it. Because the box is sealed, no one will be able to enjoy its delicious contents, let alone find the prize of great value.

Imagine if Moses had never said, "Here I am Lord." Consider if the apostle Peter had never spoken at Pentecost. Imagine if Luther had never spoken against Rome. History is replete with great happenings for the good. But you can bet that none of them was begun in silence.

There is a reason Jesus Christ is referred to as the *Word* (John 1:1-3, 14). Meaning is derived only through words. Without words, a man is reduced to a dumb brute, for he cannot even reason. Jesus Christ is the epitome of all meaning. His words are the only thing that can bring purpose, healing and wholeness to this world. And His words cannot be shared *unless they are spoken!* Indeed, as the apostle Paul asks, "...How will they believe in Him whom they have not heard? And how will they hear without a preacher?" (Romans 10:14).

What to Say and When to Say It

Many Christians get nervous in regard to sharing their faith. We hope to provide you with easy counsel so that you will never be worried about such things.

The matter of what you should say really is entirely up to you. Simply be yourself, and the rest will take care of itself. There is much you can share in the way of your faith, just like there is much to share in the way of other things that may interest you. As you grow in your faith, you will become increasingly aware that your faith and all other matters are somehow interrelated.

In time, you will come to realize the interconnectedness of topics so much that conversation regarding your convictions will become natural. In the meantime, we encourage you to observe men and women who are good at this kind of thing. Study their ways, and learn from them. There is nothing wrong with emulating them, and in fact it will be good for you to do so.

How to be a Good Conversationalist

Have you ever noticed that some people have the "gift for gab"? Such folks seem to have a natural ability to carry on conversations with acquaintances and strangers alike. Chances are good that you are already a pretty good conversationalist, but if you would like to improve your skills in this regard, then consider a couple of age old tips:

Hands down, the best way to engage in a conversation and to maintain it is to talk in terms of the other person's interests. This simply means to let the other person talk about what interests him. Don't you appreciate when others listen to what is going on in your life, or when they ask you to elaborate on something that you've already told them? Of course you do, and others do as well.

Another important factor is to maintain good eye contact and be at ease. You might include phrases in your responses which affirm to the speaker that you are listening well. Listening is an act of respect, and it is a great way to start off any talk. Indeed, the Bible confirms this very point: "This you know, my beloved brethren. But everyone must be quick to hear, slow to speak..." (James 1:19).

Getting Your Point Across

There is absolutely nothing wrong with trying to steer a conversation in the direction you want to take it. However, the proper way to do so is out of love. If your attitude is one of simply wanting to spout off knowledge, then you will be little more than a noisy gong. But if you truly want your listener to be bettered by something you know, especially in the matter of eternal affairs, then you are demonstrating a true act of love by sharing your knowledge and convictions.

So how do you steer a conversation in a particular direction? Sometimes the best way is to be direct. You might state or ask someone matter-of-factly, "Do you go to church?", or "Do you think global warming is real?", or "Hey, I noticed that gasoline is ten cents cheaper at the corner store; I thought you'd like to know," or "The Presidential veto on the abortion ban makes me frustrated—how does it make you feel?", or "What do you think about Jesus Christ?"

You will note in some of the above examples that questions are included. Questions often make people think, and thus serve to generate momentum for further discussion. Upon reply, you may sometimes find that the recipient has much in common with you, and so an existing friendship may be solidified, or a new one created.

On the flip side, you may find that certain recipients do not share your worldview, either due to ignorance, concerted decision, or a combination of the two. In these instances, we encourage you, above all else, to *engage*. How shall you do so? Above all else, be confident about the matter. Speak to convince as only you know how. Ask the Lord for wisdom and guidance in this regard, and He will surely provide according to your request.

The Great Commission

It is evident that God desires the message of His Son, Jesus, to be spread by Christians like you and me. His parting words before His ascension into heaven made this clear: "Go therefore and make disciples of all the nations, baptizing them in the name of the Father and the Son and the Holy Spirit, teaching them to observe all that I commanded you; and lo, I am with you always, even to the end of the age" (Matt. 28:19-20). This passage of Scripture is commonly known as the "Great Commission."

God does not hold you accountable for anything other than your willingness to share your faith with others. It should not be your burden whether or not someone receives the truth you have to offer. That is the Holy Spirit's job, for He is the One who convicts others of sin and of righteousness (John 16:8-9). If you will do your part, the Holy Spirit will do His, regardless of the outcome. But know that the Spirit needs you to provide proper knowledge about God to others in order for Him to do His part.

A Proper Challenge

A properly conveyed conviction will somehow also convey an appropriate challenge. By this we mean that your sentiments should often cause others to wonder if they should accept the truth that you offer. There is no one, set way of doing this, but being wimpy or shy in your approach will likely never achieve a proper effect. On the contrary, be certain about what you say.

Consider the following dialog between Nicodemus and Jesus:

... "Rabbi, we know that You have come from God as a teacher; for no one can do these signs that You do unless God is with him."

Jesus answered and said to him, "Truly, truly, I say to you, unless one is born again he cannot see the kingdom of God."

Nicodemus said to Him, "How can a man be born when he is old? He cannot enter a second time into his mother's womb and be born, can he?"

Jesus answered, "Truly, truly, I say to you, unless one is born of water and the Spirit he cannot enter into the kingdom of God. That which is born of the flesh is flesh, and that which is born of the Spirit is spirit. Do not be amazed that I said to you, 'You must be born again.' "The wind blows where it wishes and you hear the sound of it, but do not know where it comes from and where it is going; so is everyone who is born of the Spirit."

Nicodemus said to Him, "How can these things be?"

Jesus answered and said to him, "Are you the teacher of Israel and do not understand these things?

John 3:2-10

A number of key points can be gleaned from this passage. For one, Jesus was not flattered after hearing Nicodemus' initial statement; in fact He seemed to disregard it. Second, Jesus cut to the quick and let Nicodemus know that he needed to be "born again." Third, Jesus answered Nicodemus' question directly, but in doing so He gave him cause to think deeply. Fourth, Jesus challenged Nicodemus, for although Nicodemus was a teacher, he was without understanding. If you read the rest of this passage, you will notice that Jesus provided additional knowledge so that Nicodemus could be informed and properly challenged.

While on this subject, we should warn you that some Christians will erroneously tell you that you should never argue a matter with a person, for doing so might scare him away. This teaching is simply not in line with sound, biblical reason. Acts 6:9, 9:29, 11:2, 15:2-7, 17:17, 18:28, and 28:24 are just some of many passages that clearly indicate that the apostles never shied away from a debate which held the potential to influence others for the good. In these passages, we see that they "argued with," "debated with," "convinced," and "persuaded" at various points in their dialogs with others.

Choosing Your Battles

We want to make sure that you do not carry things too far and try to convince everybody of everything you think you know. So we counsel you strongly to limit your passions to truly relevant matters as they pertain to your audience. You do not need to try to convince someone that Garth Brooks is the world's best musician if that person couldn't care less about country music, nor should you try to convince someone to buy night crawlers from you if that person is truly apathetic to the matter. Your convictions may or may not have importance, but regardless—you cannot pour water into a container which has its lid on. Trying to do so may only cause a mess.

However, eternal matters are always relevant to your audience, and so it should be evident in your life that they are more important than drama, politics, business, music, sporting events, or fine food. We are not saying that these topics are not worth discussing (on the contrary!). Rather, we are stating that topics involving eternal matters, like life, death, and salvation should be interwoven into your conversations from time to time, even often.

You will do well also to not "major on the minors." In other words, don't pick a fight about small things when you and another person agree on larger points. This is especially true in regard to sharing your beliefs with other Christians who may not see eye to eye with you on every matter. If you are both in agreement with the tenets of your faith, then celebrate your friendship accordingly. It's all right to discuss minor points of dissention, but do so in an attitude whereby you both hope to be bettered by your conversations.

Proverbs tells us, "Do not reprove a scoffer, or he will hate you. Reprove a wise man and he will love you" (9:8). What is a scoffer? A scoffer is someone who sneers, mocks, or otherwise makes disrespectful remarks about your convictions. It is not wise to reprove a scoffer, so you will need to exercise keen discretion in this regard. This means you will need to identify a true scoffer and avoid him accordingly.

But you should know that not everyone who sneers at your remarks is a true scoffer. In fact, it may be common that people will respond to you in a seemingly disrespectful way, but you should not be quick to judge their response as being genuine. Truth be told, you might be convicting certain people of their sins, and so they might respond in a defensive manner. But in doing so, they might also be seriously thinking about what you have said. After all, the Bible says that the word of God is "... living and active and sharper than any two-edged sword, and piercing as far as the division of soul and spirit, of both joints and marrow, and able to judge the thoughts and intentions of the heart" (Hebrews 4:12). So take heart if someone makes comments or gestures that indicate that your words are being rejected. You may be planting seeds that will later grow.

The Worth of It All

You will sometimes find that your stated convictions are the cause for others to understand Christ, and that you are able to lead them to the Better Way! Let this be your highest hope and aim, and you will find joy immeasurable. Almost everyone who is a Christian was led into his faith by the convincing words of another person, and you have the ability to lead others into a saving faith as well. Indeed, you wield a great and wonderful strength, and there is no better way of using it than to lead another person to Jesus Christ.

Are You Ready?

So, here we are, at the end of our final lesson. Are you ready to be a man of conviction? Are you ready to be *complete in Christ?*

It is likely by now that you know that *teleo* means "complete." It is fitting then to conclude by providing you a challenge in the way of a thought provoking passage. You should already be somewhat familiar with this passage, for it involves the story of the rich young ruler that we referred to earlier:

And someone came to Him and said, "Teacher, what good thing shall I do that I may obtain eternal life?"

And He said to him, "...if you wish to enter into life, keep the commandments...."

The young man said to Him, "All these things I have kept; what am I still lacking?"

Jesus said to him, "If you wish to be complete, go and sell your possessions and give to the poor, and you will have treasure in heaven; and come, follow Me." But when the young man heard this statement, he went away grieving; for he was one who owned much property. And Jesus said to His disciples, "Truly I say to you, it is hard for a rich man to enter the kingdom of heaven...."

When the disciples heard this, they were very astonished and said, "Then who can be saved?"

And looking at them Jesus said to them, "With people this is impossible, but with God all things are possible."
Matt. 19:16-26

If you are a keen reader, you will have noticed that Jesus

challenged the rich young ruler by stating, "*If you wish to be complete*...." The word used to signify "complete" in the original Greek passage is *teleo*. Do you wish to be complete? If so, are you willing to ask Jesus, as did the young ruler, "What am I still lacking?"

Are you willing to commit and devote yourself to Jesus so much so that you will always want to know your lack so that you can have it filled for His glory? The rich young ruler asked this question, but the answer did not suit him, and so he walked away in the same grieving state he began in. May you not be like him! Instead, may you always exercise the courage to recognize that Jesus has provided for your lack, and that through Him, as the good word states, "All things are possible." Let this be your passion, your mission, and your life-long conviction.

We are honored to have spent this time with you, and honored still to continue our time, for together we will work until Jesus comes. May you be forever brave in the knowledge that He who died for you *has made you complete*!

God bless you!

Printed in the United States
147019LV00003B/4/P

9 781883 651343